THE INTERNET FOR LIBRARY AND INFORMATION SERVICE PROFESSIONALS

2nd Edition

Andy Dawson

The Aslib Know How Series

Editor : Sylvia P Webb

THE ASSOCIATION FOR INFORMATION MANAGEMENT

Published in 1997 by
Aslib, The Association for Information Management
Staple Hall, Stone House Court, London EC3A 7PB

***

British Library Cataloguing in Publication Data
A catalogue record for this book is available from the British Library
ISBN 0 85142 400 7

Aslib, The Association for Information Management, founded in 1924,
is a world class corporate membership organisation with two thousand corporate members in some 70 countries. It actively promotes
better management of information resources.

Aslib lobbies on all aspects of the management of and legislation con-
cerning information. It provides consultancy and information services, professional development training, specialist recruitment, and
publishes primary and secondary journals, conference proceedings,
directories and monographs.

Further information about Aslib can be obtained from :
Aslib, The Association for Information Management
Staple Hall, Stone House Court, London EC3A 7PB
Tel: +44 (0) 171 903 0000, Fax: +44 (0) 171 903 0011
Email aslib@aslib.co.uk, WWW http://www.aslib.co.uk/

Series Editor - Sylvia P. Webb

Sylvia Webb is a well known consultant, author and lecturer in the information management field. Her first book 'Creating an Information Service' now in its third edition was published by Aslib and has sold in over forty countries. She has experience of working in both the public and private sectors, ranging from public libraries to national and international organisations. She has also been a lecturer at Ashridge Management College, specialising in management and inter-personal skills, which led to her second book, 'Personal Development in Information Work', also published by Aslib. She has served on a number of government advisory bodies and is past Chair of the Information and Library Services Lead Body which develops National Vocational Qualifications (NVQs) for the LIS profession. She is actively involved in professional education with Aslib and the Library Association and is also a former Vice-President of the Institute of Information Scientists. As well as being editor of this series, Sylvia Webb has also written two of the Know How Guides: '*Making a charge for library and information services*' and '*Preparing a guide to your library and information service*'.

A list of titles in the Aslib Know How Series
appears on the back cover of this volume.

Acknowledgments

To all the As for their love and support

Contents

Introduction to the 2nd edition

I am very glad that this book has been successful enough to warrant a second edition, as there are a number of significant changes and additions which I have wished to make, despite less than two years passing since its first publication. It is the nature of the Internet that changes within it take place all the time. Even in the original edition I was at pains to point out the rapidity with which these changes take place, and had to take care to write it in a fashion which would minimise the negative effects of these changes on the value of the book. I think I was successful in this at the time, as much of the material included in the second edition stands unaltered from the first. However, for all that, the focus of the Internet has changed dramatically in even this short time and whilst much of the original retains its validity, there is also much which is new, or which needs expansion, particularly with reference to developments related to the use of the World Wide Web (WWW) and the tools which are used to create, view and search for resources on it.

Thus the reader of this edition will find much which is familiar, but also I hope much which is new and of additional value to assist when trying to use the resources of the Internet in an effective manner for information retrieval. The chapters which cover older systems and tools have been retained, although slightly truncated, as they all still have their occasional use and it is beneficial to be aware of how they can be applied to fulfil particular needs. The introductory section and that on email and newsgroups have been updated to include some new developments but remain predominantly as before. The chapter on the WWW has been significantly expanded and updated to include much more material on the developments in search tools, Java, agents, browser wars etc., and some further thoughts have been added to the summary. The appendix and glossary have been enlarged and updated, although throughout the philosophy has remained that of the original edition - to try to convey an understanding of the underlying strengths and weaknesses of the Internet and its tools, and to point only to key links and gateways to help the reader find information on the Internet, rather than to provide a more comprehensive listing of links which would inevitably be out of date before the book hit the streets.

1. Preface to the first edition

Why yet another book on the Internet? For several reasons. Firstly, the great majority of the many books and articles on the Internet still tend to be written with plenty of praise for the wonders of the 'net but with little mention of the problems which exist. The reality of using the Internet, particularly when using it for information retrieval, is somewhat less rosy than the view commonly presented through the tinted glasses of the media. It is very important that the current and intrinsic limitations of the Internet and the tools we use on it must be understood if we are to make effective use of them. Hopefully this book goes some way to providing that understanding through the presentation of not only the strengths of the Internet as an information resource and communications medium, but also a realistic and pragmatic view of the weaknesses and shortcomings it possesses.

Whilst there are again many books offering advice about how to use the Internet and its tools, there are virtually none which do so from the viewpoint of an information professional, whose needs, approach and (most importantly) expectations differ significantly from the common-or-garden Internet "punter". This book tries to take account of these factors and to present sound advice which answers the information worker's questions and prepares him or her with a realistic view of what can be achieved when using the Internet.

Finally, in a market stuffed with fat, expensive tomes containing much material of questionable value to the average user, there seemed to be a particular shortage of concise, reasonably-priced and sensibly-balanced works, and fewer still with particular relevance to LIS. Hopefully, this guide will fill this gap.

I suppose I could also have said "for personal fame and fortune", but as I have already promised above, this book is supposed to be realistic and pragmatic... :-)

What this book is:

A pragmatic, bottom-up basic practical guide to the use of the Internet for information retrieval, explaining the nature of the Internet, how it works, the information tools you find on it, their strengths and weaknesses, and strategies for efficient and successful use of those tools. It includes basic theory which is important for proper understanding, but it is also shares tried and tested practical solutions to common problems. It includes many ideas and pointers to help you locate the sources and methods which are most likely to be beneficial to your particular needs and to avoid some of the obvious pitfalls, and suggests philosophies of use to maximise the potential benefits of Internet use whilst minimising the drawbacks.

What this book is not:

This book does not seek to be a complete, reference work on the Internet. There are plenty of those around already. If you want recommendations for such a text, see the Further Reading section in the back of this book. Nor is it intended to be a technical manual, or a step-by step guide to setting up Internet connections and tools. Perhaps most importantly, this book does not contain, nor ever could, a comprehensive and up-to-date list of resources in the LIS field although it does provide *some.* It concentrates rather on giving information on how to *find* such resources, and identifies many of the more mainstream starting points. Hopefully, if you read on, you will come to understand why this has to be the case.

Who should definitely read this book:

LIS workers and professionals who:

- want to understand what the Internet is and how it works
- want to know more about the potential of the Internet as an information source
- want to know what search tools are available and how they work
- are already using the Internet for information retrieval and want to do so more effectively
- are experiencing frustration and failure when trying to find information on the Internet
- want to get to grips with the terminology of the Internet

Who this book is probably inappropriate for:

- Technical experts looking for technical detail
- Those seeking assistance in setting up physical connections to the Internet

2. The nature of the Internet

What is the Internet?

Especially in these days of umpteen Internet magazines, Internet columns in the daily papers, and even the BBC networking club, the question "what is the Internet" may seem a superfluous one. Doesn't everybody already know? Well, yes, in a sense; the great majority of people are probably now aware of the *existence* of the Internet, but that's not quite the same thing. Many people have perhaps a somewhat misguided view of what the Internet really is, certainly as far as it affects information retrieval. And a proper understanding of what it is makes a big difference to how we might view our use of it and the typical problems we might encounter.

In essence, it's probably easiest to see the Internet in two related but distinct parts: the *communications network*, the immense web of interconnected local and wide area networks, telephone lines, cables, fibre-optics and (even) satellite links which provide the medium for the transfer of information around the Internet, and the *computers* and computing sites which actually hold and process the data which is available to be transmitted across the network. Now, whilst the communications network part of things is extremely well integrated, and for the most part operates transparently to the user, the same cannot be said for the data end of the business.

The communications network is basically a physical network of connections, "wires" if you like (although much of it is not "wired" in the traditional sense, but uses optical cable or even non-physical transmission media such as radio or microwave bands) which provide the means of passing signals from one place to another. What makes it so easy to use is the adoption of a common set of *protocols*, or standard "ways of talking", which enable data to be passed coherently and easily from one place on the network to another. TCP/IP (Transmission Control Protocol/Internet Protocol) is at the heart of the Internet's communications; think of it as being common language and rules for behaviour in the communications environment, which all parts of the Internet share and understand. All the computer systems connected to the Internet have to be able to the TCP/IP "language" to communicate - or have something (a communications program or stack) to interpret and translate for them. Because of the universality of this well-defined language, the protocol, everyone on the Net can communicate easily with everyone else. Even better, we the users don't really have to know anything about how TCP/IP works - we don't give it instructions directly - it just sits there behind the scenes and gets on with things once it's been set up. We can talk in our local "dialect", use Windows, DOS, UNIX, whatever, and programs will take care of translating anything we want to send across the net into a form which complies with the protocol.

But we have to remember that this common language is concerned with one thing and one thing only - communication. All it does is make it easy for one machine to contact another, to be able to pass data from one place to another. It has nothing to do with controlling, specifying or standardising the content of data which may be transmitted. And this is where the problems start to occur. What makes the communications side of the operation work so well is the extent of the standardisation, the agreement on a universal common code. When it comes to the specification, organisation, searching and retrieval of data on computers around the world, however, the idea of a universal standard goes straight out of the window. There is no global standard for the organisation or description of information, which inevitably means that identifying and retrieving material is considerably more fraught with difficulty than the action of simply moving it about across the net. In my experience, information workers tend to experience particular problems and disappointment in the area of information retrieval from the Internet, because they have been used to working with information that is organised, or which they are responsible for organising; and when faced with a body of information which is *inherently disorganised*, they find it difficult to come to terms with - hence the many well-intentioned but doomed and pointless calls for projects to "index the Internet". You can't ultimately index the Internet, ever - it's too big, too fluid and too diverse.

Fortunately, there are a number of widely-used tools which require certain common elements in the description and organisation of data for Internet access, such as gopher, WAIS and most prominently these days, the World Wide Web (WWW). Whilst these tools create some degree of standardisation which benefits the searcher, they still leave something to be desired. We shall look in more detail at these systems and their strengths and weaknesses later in the book. For now, let us just remember that there are inherent problems with information organisation and retrieval over the Internet, and take a look at some of the other basics.

Where did it come from?

The Internet was originally developed from work which was done for the US Department of Defence who, during the Cold War years, were concerned that in the event of a nuclear attack, their communications system could be knocked out by a very small number of missiles hitting key communications centres. Thus they set about developing a *distributed* system, which could withstand the destruction of any number of its component *nodes* and still remain functional. The benefits of this approach were readily apparent, and its use extended from government research into academia. However, outside major academic and research institutions, computing provision did not allow access to the Internet for anyone but the relatively privileged until the explosion of microcomputing, which provided the mass home market which commercial providers sought to tap by selling connections to the masses. Currently the original, predominantly academic community of Internet users is being flooded by the exponential growth of new users from the private sector, whose needs, desires and expectations (not to mention wallets) are rather different from those of the established order. Whilst much material is still mounted on machines in universities and colleges, there is an enormous acceleration in the provision of materials by commercial concerns and even by private individuals.

Technicalities- how does it work?

Communications
In simple terms, the Internet works by breaking down all information which needs to be transmitted into *packets* which contain not only the data to be transmitted, but also information about where it has to go, where it came from, and what other packets of data it relates to. Because these packets are in a standard form, and a standard method of addressing is used for them, they can be passed from any "Internet-aware" point on the network to the next until they reach their destination.

An analogy with the traditional postal service is quite helpful here. Imagine you lived in London and you wanted to send a letter to your friend in Los Angeles by post. You would write your letter, put it in an envelope, write your friend's name and address on the envelope, put yours on the back, and deliver it to the nearest postbox. From the postbox, a postman would collect the letters and take them to the local post office, where they would be sent on to the nearest main post office and sorted. From there your letter would be sent to the airport, put on a plane and flown across the Atlantic, and be delivered at the other end first to a main post office, then sent on to a local post office, then taken by a postman and delivered to your friend's mailbox. This is exactly what happens with your electronic data; your local software puts your data into an electronic "envelope" and sends it to the computer which handles your connection. It reads the address and passes your data on to a point or node higher up the communications chain, and eventually across the Atlantic on a main route to a main point at the other end, then down a chain to a local "post office" and finally to your friend's own postbox.

You could equally use the analogy of travelling by road, using local roads from your house to a junction with a B road, then to a junction with an A road, then to a junction with the motorway, then up the motorway to the other end of the country, then off the motorway and back down the A and B roads and finally to the door at the other end. This is a nice analogy as, if there were roadworks on the motorway and it was closed, you could detour off via some other roads, pass the blockage, and get back on the motorway afterwards. This is again exactly what happens to traffic on the Internet: it takes the most direct route that is available, but can be re-routed through any available pathway if necessary. The only difference between these processes and what actually happens is that your electronic message is split into independently-transmitted parts (the packets), rather than being sent as a whole, if it's more than a certain size. You can think of this as the equivalent of splitting your letter into separate pages, numbering each page, and sending each page in its own envelope. Your friend can then receive the pages in any order, via different routes if necessary, and reassemble them into your letter at his end; and since you numbered them all, if one failed to arrive he could ask you to send that page again. By breaking transmission into these standard data packets, transmission across the Internet is made as efficient and robust as possible.

Client/server concepts

One of the most important concepts in Internet information provision is the idea of *client/server architecture*. Almost every net-based tool relies on this basic approach in order to be able to function efficiently; and it is important that we understand how it works, as it can have a direct effect on how we search and the results we retrieve. Fortunately, the client/server model is a simple one. As its name implies, it is constituted of two parts, two programs, a client and a server, for each application. The *client* software runs on the *local* machine, the PC on our desk perhaps. The *server* software runs on another machine, perhaps a mainframe, the host or server of the information we want to retrieve. The application works by the combination of both pieces of software working co-operatively together. A client without a server, or a server with no clients, would do nothing useful. Software tools for client/server systems always work in pairs, and share the computing workload.

The server program is responsible for holding the data which is to be made available, and for finding and returning data requested by the clients. Typically it is responsible for creating indexes, searching, and sometimes collecting and organising data. Most importantly, it provides the means of allowing common access to the data mounted on it. It waits for client software to send it requests to do something, and returns the results of its efforts in response to such requests.

The client program is responsible for dealing with the user. It runs locally, and provides the interface between the user and the system, collecting information about what the user wants, transforming the requests into the agreed language of communication between the client and the server, packaging them up and sending them off to the relevant server computer. When the server responds with some data, the client "unpacks" the coded material and converts it for appropriate display and/or filing at the user's machine.

One of the key benefits of this sort of system is that communications between the client and server do not need to be continuous; they can be intermittent. There is no need to maintain a connection between the client and the server, since the client's "message" to the server to, say, perform a search and return the results, is self-contained. The client is like the user's secretary, taking an interactive part in noting down what is wanted, checking that all the information is there, and then writing out and sending the instructions to achieve the desired result. Once the message is composed and sent, the client's machine can do something else whilst it waits for the response. Likewise, the server simply waits for instructions from clients to be passed to it, acts on them on receipt, and returns answers. Although acting co-operatively, the client and server act independently. This *asynchronous* form of communication ensures that local, remote and communications resources are all used as efficiently as possible, without waiting for each other and tying up resources which could be used for other purposes or by other users; and it is ideally suited to the packet-switched nature of Internet communications.

Another important benefit of the client/server architecture is that different clients and servers can be developed which will still work together. So long as they understand the requirements for the "language" of the requests and responses to be transmitted between them, clients and servers which act in totally different ways locally can be developed. This is why there are for example many competing programs which act as World Wide Web (WWW) browsers: Netscape, Explorer, Mosaic, Lynx, Cello, Winweb, Macweb, Internetworks, each of which have different local functionality, look different, can run under different operating systems, but all of which can access WWW resources. Thus it is easier to communicate across different systems with client/server architecture, and also for suppliers to develop and compete with alternative products. For each application, the client and server will speak the same language for communication of what they want each other to do, as well as using Internet protocols for transmitting the requests and responses back and forth.

Types of connection
It is important to be aware that there are different kinds of connection to the Internet which substantially affect the way in which we will be able to work on it. There are two fundamental methods of connection: full connection or terminal connection.

Full connection actually makes the machine you are working at a part of the Internet. It is established either by direct connection, typically used by universities and corporate users, where a machine or network of machines is permanently linked by dedicated line to the net, and has its own address; or remotely by using SLIP (Serial Line Internet Protocol) or PPP (Point to Point Protocol) connections to a directly connected machine or *router*. With full connection, you can install any client software you like on your machine and use all the facilities of the net.

Terminal connection is where your local computer connects to another (host) computer which has a full connection, but acts only as a *terminal* on the host machine. The local computer is not part of the Internet: you simply use it to log on to the host, and then access the Internet from the (connected) host. There are three key differences to your working practice which result from these different types of connection. Firstly, with a terminal connection, your viewing is limited to the type of communication between yourself and the host, which is usually a text only link. If you want to use a graphic browser like Netscape and view pictures, you can't do it from a simple terminal connection (unless your host provides some special client/ server software, which is unusual). Secondly, since it is the host machine you are actually working from (the host is doing all the processing, your local computer is just a terminal on that machine), you are limited to running the specific applications which are provided by the host. Thirdly, all the data you see and request is delivered to and stored on the host, not your local machine. If you want to hold or use the data on your machine, you must first transfer it from the host by a separate process. Likewise if you want to send data from your machine to somewhere else on the net, you must first send it to your host; only then can it be passed onto the Internet. By implication, you must have an account on the host machine to use a terminal connection: although there are some sites (known as public access sites) which allow anyone to dial in and use certain facilities on their machines (see under resource guides in the appendix for some of these). Most commercial access suppliers providing terminal access provide an *off-line mail reader*, a program which lets you fetch email from the host and send back mail you have previously written locally, off-line, with a minimum of fuss (and connect time!).

It is the norm today for commercial hosts to provide SLIP/PPP connections, but not all do, especially those in areas where telecommunications facilities are poor and the Internet is still developing, e.g. many African countries, so make sure you know what you're getting if you're signing up. Also, be aware that configuring your system to run a SLIP or PPP connection isn't necessarily a simple task. The "Internet in a box" type of package, which sells you preconfigured, self-installing software plus a subscription to a service provider, can certainly help the technically inexperienced in setting up a full connection, but it's not always foolproof. Although the sorts of package provided by major Online Service Providers (OSPs - who offer charged data services as well as basic connectivity, and usually charge by the hour) like America Online (AOL) and CompuServe are fully self-installing and pretty reliable, many of the smaller Internet Service Providers (ISPs - who only provide connectivity and basic services such as email and web servers, and typically have flat-rate monthly fees) do not offer such reliable "black box" setups when you sign up.

Data problems on the Internet

The organisation of data
There are tens of millions of computers connected to the Internet, and many of them hold (and are prepared to share) information which is of potential value. However, it is vital to remember that in the majority of cases this data is assembled, organised and held *in the first instance* for local use, not for the public; it is only offered to the public as an afterthought, a secondary gesture. Take for example a university. It will probably have a CWIS (Campus-Wide Information System) through which it might provide a number of facilities: access to its library, information on courses, local information, and pointers to other sources, other sites, where information which might be useful is stored. These databases will be mounted, formatted and made accessible in whatever forms and through whatever tools the site deems most suitable and helpful *for its own users* - and quite rightly so. Only in the area of commercial and industrial services is it generally true that information providers are intending their information to go out to the public at large as a primary purpose. Thus data which might be quite meaningful in its original organisational context is

actually most unhelpful when retrieved outside that context. Take as an example course unit information. Searches for information on broad topics (e.g. archaeology) will often retrieve many references to such course units, which would make perfect sense if you were searching locally to see what courses were running, but which simply generate noise if you are looking for subject information. Even if you *want* to find a course to attend, you could have difficulties, as many of these entries do not include information about the institution which is offering them! Ridiculous? Not really - as we have said, these institutions are providing local information first, and local users searching local resources know where the course is being run - locally! The problem only arises when remote searches are made.

Another outcome of this approach is that things may well not be organised in a consistent manner, or even accessible in a consistent manner. In practice, the former is more often true than the latter, as much information has been made accessible through tools like Gopher, FTP and the Web, which being so easy to acquire and set up, as well as being effective tools for local information dissemination, have become standards de facto. This is helpful to us as searchers after information, although we are still enormously hampered by the lack of agreement in conceptual organisation and description of data - more on this later.

A further natural outcome is that many places want many things in common, and recognise that it is inefficient to reinvent the wheel. Therefore, they look for other sites which already have the sorts of resource they would like, and try to capitalise on those existing resources. As a result, many of the things which are found on the Internet are not actually original data themselves, but *pointers*, references to data held elsewhere. This is, of course, very efficient for the local sites; but it has major ramifications for searching (and, ultimately, for the provision of "free" information over the Internet).

Firstly, it means that increasing numbers of places will typically have references to the same "good" sites' data. This inevitably means more people try to use the same resources; which means more delays due to congestion, and poorer service for both distant (and more importantly, local) users. As the external traffic grows and slows down the system for local as well as remote users, what does the provider do? Upgrade the system to handle the increased, largely external, load? Will these external people pay for this? As the volume of users on the Internet grows, so more and more key sites are starting to restrict, commercialise, or even shut down their "services to the public". This commercialisation is currently supported in the main by advertising - which further adds to the congestion problem, presenting millions of users with graphic adverts which 99.99% of the time they have no interest in. In my view, this also runs the risk of dissatisfied advertisers "pulling the plug" and undermining the ability of major search services to continue to provide large-scale "free" search services. Why should they become dissatisfied, I hear you ask? Although largely anecdotal, there is plenty of evidence to suggest that users have an uncanny ability to "blank out" such adverts when they're searching - as the market becomes more mature and the relative weakness of such advertising becomes evident, funding may well switch into more productive forms of advertising.

Secondly, and very importantly for searchers, it means that different places will have what amounts to the same "information" - or more specifically, different pointers to the same information. However, it is not always easy to tell what is the same and what is different; if you search for something, you search (normally) for a descriptive word being used in conjunction with a thing. On different sites, pointers to the same actual piece of data may be described identically, or similarly, or dissimilarly; and likewise, different real data may be described identically, or similarly, or dissimilarly. Searches may return large numbers of similar or different hits, but it can be very difficult to easily ascertain which are duplications and which are not. Some of these problems and other related ones, particularly with regard to web-based search engines, are addressed further in the WWW chapter.

The volume and quality of data
Another, different problem of retrieval from the Internet is that of the sheer volume of data involved, as well as their distributed nature. The concept of "information overload" is not a new one - it has been with us for decades - but it has perhaps never been more true than in the case of Internet-based information. An individual mailing list may generate as many as a hundred messages a day; and there are thousands of mailing lists, not to mention newsgroups. There are millions of computers hosting accessible, retrievable information to the Internet user. Apart from the immediate problem of accurately identifying the sort of data the user wants in this morass of information which, as we have already discussed, is so inherently disorganised, there are two other critical difficulties.

Unlike other electronic forms of data supply, traditional "online" services which were provided on a commercial basis with the concomitant need for (and implication of) a degree of quality, accuracy and reliability of information sold, the great majority of information available via the Internet is still "free"- that is, there is no explicit charge for data retrieved. So, why do people make data available on the Internet?

Remembering the roots of the Net in academia and research as a means of sharing information, it is easy to see that much of what is available stems from this original mentality. Many of the most important information sites, resources and tools have come from (and continue to come from) the academic sector and a genuine sense of altruism, of doing things for the greater good. Many commercial providers offer limited "free" services as a come-on for their paid services; take shareware, for example, which is becoming increasingly popular. Commercial providers are also increasingly seeing web pages as a form of corporate or brand-awareness tool as well as an opportunity for online sales, and many more pages are now corporate sites doing little more than staking an Internet presence. More and more, interestingly, are starting to follow a "sponsoring" line - providing pages on a "fun" topic (which they might expect many users to visit) unrelated to their core business (which far fewer users would search for) and simply badging them with their names. But the biggest growth in Internet information provision has been in the form of personal contributions, from enthusiasts providing quality sites through dedicated effort, to people creating web pages "because everybody else is doing it", to the archives of discussion lists and newsgroups. An enormous volume of the data on the Internet is now produced by individuals with no controls on the quality or accuracy of the material they provide - and precious little comeback for those who might misguidedly rely on their data. Whilst the experienced net user can become quite adept at provenancing specific data and assessing its probable worth, there is no technical or reliable method for assessing the quality or accuracy of any piece of data retrieved from the Internet, and despite the many cries for the development of such a tool it remains a practical impossibility for network resources as a whole.

The revisions of data
The other critical problem arising from the volume of data available ties back to the fact that, as we have noted, many of the data items found on the Internet are not actually source data, but merely pointers to such data. Let us hypothesise for a moment. Imagine there are ten million information-providing sites on the Internet - a very conservative figure in all probablility. Let us assume that each of those sites holds a mere thousand data items - again, on average, quite conservative. Finally, let us assume that an item of data has an average life of about 3 years before it is renamed, deleted or otherwise relocated or removed from its original resting place - in reality, an extremely conservative estimate! You do not need to be a mathematical genius to work out that this equates to TEN MILLION DOCUMENTS A DAY

undergoing modifications which change their ultimate physical location. Even if you wish to be more conservative with the original figures, it is clear that hundreds of thousands of items a day must be affected. Since, as we have discussed, these items are often *referenced* by others, and since these references are unidirectional - that is the link only exists from the reference to the document, not from the document to the reference - it immediately becomes clear that the number of out-of-date references and links to materials on the Internet must be staggering. No matter how careful site owners are in checking and rechecking the validity and currency of links (even using the various tools which try to assist in this task - and, inevitably, add further to the congestion problem by repeatedly following links to see if they still work - which are becoming more widespread), it is inevitable that many links are going to be invalid when they come to be followed. Once more, this is a problem to which there is currently no good solution; it is simply something which needs to be understood and expected. When you try to retrieve material from the Internet and receive an error message, the odds are it's not because of a system failure, or user error, or congestion; it's simply because the reference is out-of-date.

So what does this mean for the information professional trying to find a specific piece of information on the net? It may seem that I have painted a very black picture of the state of information retrieval on the Internet. If so, all well and good - because these are real problems for the information worker, which we must be aware of, and which are all too often glossed over by the media hype. But I'm not trying to say that effective information retrieval is impossible on the Internet - far from it. I'm simply trying to make it clear that we're playing in a different ballpark from the cosy, organised, indexed, coded, managed, controlled environment which we are used to as information workers, when we work with the Internet. If we simply expect to be able to transplant our traditional approaches into this new environment, we will be disappointed by the results. We have to learn to accept the Internet for what it is, and learn how to play the game by its rules. For it is only when we do this, that we will be able to avoid disappointment, play a good game, and win out in the end.

So let's now move on to take a look at the specific tools of the Internet and see how we can best play the game!

3. Email, lists and newsgroups

Email and the Internet

The most pervasive and basic of Internet activities is electronic mail, or email. Whilst in its simplest form, it stands as an electronic replacement for the traditional postal service, it also encompasses a number of far more powerful capabilities which can be of great use to the information professional. The power and value of email is easily overlooked in these days of focus on the "prettier" parts of the Internet, i.e. the WWW, but an enormous amount can be achieved with this most basic of tools. A fully detailed look at the capabilities of electronic mail would fill a book such as this on its own - and indeed does, in the shape of Simon Pride's know-how guide Email for Librarians (see further reading) - so this section of the book concentrates on some key activities and uses of email and email-related resources of most potential use to the information worker.

Firstly, of course, in its role as a substitute for postal communication, email provides an excellent opportunity for the rapid and cheap exchange of ideas, questions and answers. Email "letters" are delivered in moments, rather than days, even to the other side of the world. This allows electronic "conversations" to take place with ease (quite apart from the real-time text exchange facilities provided by tools such as IRC - Internet Relay Chat) and greatly facilitates a question-and-answer process between individuals. And let us never forget, it is peoples' knowledge which is usually the greatest resource which we can tap. If we know "experts" on the net, it is an extremely simple matter to drop them an electronic line to ask for an opinion, a fact, or an answer. But although email makes this kind of interpersonal information-seeking easy, we first need (of course) to know who and where these experts are in order to ask our questions.

Mailing lists

The mailing list is a very natural extension of the simple process of email exchange, and one which can greatly support the information worker in the enquiry process. To understand the way a mailing list works, let's use a simple analogy. Imagine you are interested in gardening, and you have a group of half-a-dozen friends who also have this interest. You agree to share any good gardening tips you get with each other. With only half-a-dozen of you, each of you could ring round the others if you hear something new and useful. But what happens if others want to join, or if people leave, or move house? In anything but the smallest group, things have to be formalised into a club, and someone given the job of being a secretary, who keeps a record of who the members are and who acts as a focal point for the receipt and distribution of information from and to the club's members.

Small groups of people often use personal email to communicate informally between themselves on a given topic of shared interest, just as our friends above did. But as soon as such groups grow and feel the need to formalise, they switch to a mailing list. Although this requires one of them to act as a nominal "owner" for the list, the "secretarial" work of record-keeping and handling incoming and outgoing mail is done automatically by a piece of email *list server* software. Running on a host machine somewhere on the net, it maintains the list of members, deals with adding and deleting new and resigned members, redistributes incoming mail to all the current list members , and so forth. Servers can be set up to handle single lists, but commonly lists are handled at main sites which maintain hundreds (and in some cases, thousands) of lists.

From a user's point of view, a mailing list is very simple. You send a message to the server which hosts the list you're interested in asking to join. Once you're on the list, you will receive a copy of every piece of email which anyone submits to that list, automatically. You too can send material to a list (whether you are a member of it or not) which will be forwarded on to all the other members. The address of a server might be

    mailbase@mailbase.ac.uk

and that of a list on that server might be

    lis-link@mailbase.ac.uk

Note that the locational part of the address (the bit after the @ sign) is the same, but the name part is different for the server and the list. This is something which people often get mixed up, but it's really very simple; if you want to address the members, send your mail to the list name, and if you want to talk to administration, send to the server name. So (for instance) if asking to join or leave, send to the server (mailbase@); if contributing to discussions, send to the list (lis-link@).

Not every list is immediately accessible to the public. Lists may be *open* or *closed* lists, which means that either all applications to join the list are accepted automatically (open) or that applications to join are subject to approval by the list owners. Closed lists are relatively few in number, and tend to concern either specific research-type projects with clearly-defined memberships, or groups who are concerned about "noise" from non-expert, non-specialist or simply antagonistic others amongst the net community. If you try to join a closed list, you will receive a message from the server either referring you to someone to apply to or informing you that your application has been passed on. Also, lists may be *moderated* or *unmoderated*. An unmoderated list simply echoes every contribution, however inappropriate, repetitive or banal, to every member of the list, automatically. A moderated list has an editor who vets incoming material and only passes on deemed appropriate to members. The majority of lists are unmoderated, as of course moderating a list, particularly a busy one, is a time-consuming, unpaid job. Many people resist moderation in principle as being a form of censorship. However, good moderated lists are amongst the best sources of information on the Internet in their subject areas, and not having to wade through dozens of trashy postings every day in search of the odd jewel is something people can soon come to appreciate.

Mailing lists are extremely valuable to information workers on two counts. Firstly, they provide lots of up-to-date information and discussion on topics of particular interest - a free current awareness service, if you like. There are many knowledgeable and committed people out there, and information spreads like wildfire on the net - it's often the place you can get to hear things first. Secondly, lists give you immediate access not to just one or two experts but often to hundreds, and also allow you to cast a net for help or information with a minimum of effort - and to find the exact answer you were looking for when conventional means proved useless.

Let me give you an example from my own experience. I had a very old Apple computer (a 1980 vintage!) which I was still using for useful work and which broke down. I pulled out yellow pages and tried a number of local computer shops, none of which were prepared to look at such an old machine. I contacted Apple themselves, who suggested some specialist repairers, but they again could not help because of the age of the machine. So I went looking for mailing lists related to Apple computer users, found a general Apple systems list, and sent a message asking for suggestions. Not only did I find two people willing to do repairs, but I also got the offer of several old machines for cannibalisation!

Although this is a computing example, it is typical of the nature of mailing lists. General library-oriented lists such as lis-link frequently contain cries for help from people with information problems, and it is quite acceptable nettiquette to make such requests, so long as they're on-topic with the list's interests. At time of writing, there is even a specialist list, Stumpers-L (founded by masochistic information workers no doubt), which is specifically for people to send difficult questions to! Perhaps the most suprising thing is that, despite the increasingly prevalent what's-in-it-for-me commercialism of modern society, Internet mailing lists provide a last bastion of altruism, with an astonishing number of people being only too willing to invest considerable time in providing you with the most copious answers, asking nothing more in return than that you consider helping another user in like fashion if you have the knowledge and opportunity. This co-operative spirit is one of the joys of using the Internet, and I would urge any reader not to hesitate in replying to a question posed on a list if they have an answer. Mailing lists work because of the reciprocal efforts of their members, each contributing as he or she can, and if you join this community, you should adopt this ethic.

Mail archives

There is also an extremely valuable spin-off for information professionals from the activities of mailing lists. Being as they are foci for discussion of current and problematic aspects of whatever subject matter they are concerned with, the body of discussion which the combined mailings represent becomes in itself an extremely rich and valuable information resource.

Nearly all list servers keep archives of postings to the mailing lists they support. The periods of retention vary from server from server (and in some cases from list to list) but one year's postings is a typical figure. Not only are these archives kept for people to browse through, however, but also you can search some of them as a full-text resource! This will normally mean accessing the site through another tool, such as WAIS or via a WWW interface (described later), but is a very valuable method of identifying information on specific topics.

Additionally, many list owners keep consolidated archives of their lists for periods past their servers' retention dates. Not many of these are actively searchable, but if you are interested in older material of an active group, post a message asking about it. You can usually reach the owner of a list by posting to *listname*-request@*site*, substituting the appropriate list name and site address.

Newsgroups

Another neglected aspect of email as an information resource are newsgroups. In many ways, newsgroups are similar to mailing lists, in that they are supported by servers, and provide groups of like-minded people with a common interest to exchange information on their chosen topic. The big difference between a newsgroup and a mailing list is that mailing lists actively disseminate information, whilst newsgroups do so passively. If you join a mailing list, all contributions are sent to you automatically - you get your own copy of everything, which you can discard if you don't want. With a newsgroup, you must look to see what is available at any moment in time, and actively select what you want to see. The analogy of the newsgroup is that of the noticeboard, where you can pin up things for others to see, but they must choose to visit when your notice is up if they're going to read it, rather than the "club" analogy we used for the mailing list where things are always distributed to all members at all times.

This "passivity" is perhaps one major reason why newsgroups are often not thought of as useful information resources - it is far easier to miss things in a newsgroup than it is on a mailing list. However perhaps the biggest reason for the frequent exclusion of newsgroups as a serious information resource is something far less objective - the popular image of newsgroups as being frivolous, irreverent, temporal and (therefore) unimportant.

It is indeed extremely difficult to argue against the generalisation that newsgroups frequently contain postings which are less serious, less academic, and on more - shall we say, unusual? - topics than the average postings to mailing lists. Any brief scan through the listings of active Usenet newsgroups in the alt hierarchy, for instance, revealing such delights as alt.personals.aliens (for people who believe they're from other planets - yes really), alt.barney-the-dinosaur.die.die.die (for those who don't like Barney the dinosaur), alt.conspiracy.jfk (guess what), and alt.sex.bestiality.gerbils.duct-tape (don't ask), would give much credence to such a viewpoint. But whilst there is typically much more "frivolity" in the newsgroup community, it would be quite wrong to assume this of all groups. Firstly, many of the more outrageous groups are actually perfectly serious about their topics. This might be a very unsettling thought, but also a useful one for the day you're actually asked for an informed opinion on an outlandish or taboo subject. Secondly, there are many perfectly mainstream groups out there; it's just that newsgroups like comp.internet.library, with its discussions about where to get the best online bibliographies, simply doesn't compete well for media attention with alt.sex.pictures and lurid stories of children gaining easy access to pornography on the net. Newsgroups are certainly a more volatile arena than mailing lists on the whole, but most of the strengths of mailing lists are equally true of newsgroups - once you've found the right ones.

Finding resources in your area of interest

Which of course leads us to the inevitable, and crucial, question - how do you find a mail list/newsgroup that's relevant to your topic? Fortunately, there are a number of "lists of lists" and searchable indexes produced (see resource list in the appendix) which can be searched for that elusive topic, and most main servers provide useful access tools to the lists they provide. The most useful of these actually allow a keyword search of the contents of "information" files associated with the lists which typically describe their purpose, membership and range of discussion, but all will send a simple list of the lists they serve and the information files they have in response to an email request to the server - the command to get a list of lists is "lists" (tricky, huh?). On some servers (e.g. Mailbase) you can get brief descriptions of these lists too by adding the option "full" (lists full). Otherwise you can get further information on specific lists with the command "index *listname*". Also, running searches with some of the tools described later in this book will often turn up information files on newsgroups and lists, or references to them.A number of major sites now also provide web interfaces to their list server information (e.g. Mailbase again) with full-text search capability across descriptions as well as list names, and also of the text of messages. There is no "official" central list - although several of the "lists of lists" like to think they are! The biggest and most established sites I have found are Liszt (for mail lists) and Deja News (for newsgroups), details of which appear in the resource list appendix.

Although it's not only related to email, this seems an appropriate point to mention the Internet Public Library, and the UK based, EARL-sponsored Ask A Librarian projects, which although accessible a number of means, takes email queries and refers them to real, volunteer library and information professionals for answers. The IPL has continued to grow since its inception, and thankfully has defied my personal fears that it would become a victim of its own popularity. It has expanded considerably from this original premise to include an ever-wider range of web-based information services, but remains an excellent clearing house for requests or difficult questions of any nature. For contact details, once again see the resource list entry in the appendix.

Other considerations

A factor commonly overlooked by newcomers to email is that it was designed to work with ASCII text. This means that email messages always have to be in plain text and cannot incorporate formatting, font changes etc. which are so common in word-processing. It is however possible to send non-ASCII documents via email by *encoding* them in some way. Traditionally this is done by a process called Uuencoding, which converts the non-ASCII data into ASCII. This produces something which looks like garbage, but of course isn't; you simply have to decode it to get the original back. The point is that, if you retrieve a message which *looks* like garbage, it may well not be. A give-away is normally a line which is readable above the mess which will say "begin ...." followed by a filename. If you see such a line, you need to *Uudecode* the file to see the real thing. For more details on how to accomplish this process, take a look at Simon Pride's book or any good general Internet reference book.

An alternative method much used by windows-based mailers is to *attach* non-ASCII files to an ASCII "carrier" message. These attached messages can also be encoded, but carry information which allows the receiving mailer to know what to do with the file; usually it simply puts it away in a local directory for you to look at and use at your leisure. Of course, if you don't know about that function, it can be easy to seemingly "lose" information you have actually received. A further problem of this method is that, if your mail package differs from that used by the sender and *doesn't* use the same techniques, this automatic processing won't work. If you have a choice, use a package which supports MIME (Multipurpose Internet Mail Extensions), which is the protocol most commonly used for this sort of operation.

Apart from getting lists and running searches on remote mail servers, there are usually many other useful things they can do for you in response to simple emailed commands. If you find a server and are having trouble with it, or want to know more, try sending it a command "send info" or just "help" (to the server address). You should get back a command listing and/or some other information which will help you to proceed.

Finally, a mail management point. Many people sign up to lots of lists, get deluged with information, and feel somehow driven to scan through *every* message they receive "just in case" they miss something. DON'T! Scan the subject lines, and throw away all those that don't look useful. Most mail packages also have lots of useful tools for searching through and sorting incoming mail, but very few people take the time to work out how to use them. Familiarise yourself with the capabilities of your mailer, use them to filter your mail, and then be ruthless with it! In my view it's far better to subscribe to a wider range of groups and throw a lot of it away unread than to limit your subscriptions but read a lot of irrelevant material. Don't fall prey to the worry that you might miss something crucial. Even if you do miss something this way, if it's that important, it'll crop up again. Learn to manage your incoming mail and you can do a lot more with your time.

Key tips for the effective use of email-based resources

- Use mailing lists as a source of expert problem-solvers
- BUT don't abuse their goodwill!
- And reciprocate when you are able!
- Don't forget newsgroups, a "voluble but valuable" resource
- Use lists for current awareness information
- Utilise list and group archives as an information source
- Find the list you want through lists of lists and server searches, especially Liszt and Deja News
- Send a one-word message "help" to mailservers for assistance on their commands
- Manage your mail - don't fall prey to the "gotta read everything" syndrome
- Remember servers can supply much information in response to simple emailed commands
- Don't forget email works in ASCII only - check for other files encoded or attached
- If you're stuck, email Stumpers-L or the Internet Public Library or Ask A Librarian.

4. Telnet, Hytelnet and remote login

One of the fundamental operations perfomed on the Internet is remote login, where your own computer connects to another elsewhere on the network as if it were a terminal on that machine: in other words, as the name suggests, you are logging in to the other machine from a distance, or remotely. This allows you to work as though you were actually present at the site of the host computer, and to use all its facilities - assuming of course you have been granted the right to use them!

Telnet

Remote login is normally performed on the Internet by use of the Telnet protocol. There are various Telnet clients available with different local capabilities and options, but they all fulfil the same basic functions of providing access to remote machines by making the host machine treat their requests as if they were a local terminal on that system. However, don't make the mistake of thinking that having a Telnet client and the address of another system means you can do what you like on that system, all Telnet does for you is to make it your local machine seem to be a terminal on the host machine - as if you were there trying to log on locally. When you first connect to a host system, you will have to log in, and if you're telnetting to a site you have no rights to use, you won't be allowed to use it!

So why is Telnet so important, particularly in the library and information world, if we can't log in without permission? After all, how many of us have accounts at more than one location on the net? Because in fact the great majority of sites do let "strangers" log in to their systems, with certain restrictions. Although you won't be able to do all the things a normal account holder would be able to do, you will be able to log in to many systems as a "guest" of some sort to access publicly available material, or using a special password to grant you access to a particular type of service from the host. There are many public access sites which allow anyone to use their facilities; and services such as Archie, FTP, and Gophers at many sites also use a form of "standard log-in" for anyone who wants to use their resources. And perhaps most importantly from an information worker's point of view, almost every Internet site which has a library with an automated system will let us browse its catalogue in this way.

We Telnet to a site by giving the site address to our Telnet client and letting it make the connection for us. Once connected, we will be faced with whatever prompt a user at that site would get locally, in order to identify ourselves. Sometimes, sites have a separate address for the library; and the more helpful ones suggest to us which login to use if we want to access it. If in doubt, the obvious guess is often as not the right one: so if you want the library try logging in as "library" if no instructions are given.

When you have logged on, you will be talking to whatever OPAC or other interface the system owners have chosen to use. When you are using Telnet, you cannot select your own interface for searching through other libraries' catalogues (although with the continuing growth of the Z39.50 standard, this may commonly be possible in the not too distant future) - you're using the software on their machine, and your machine is simply acting as a terminal on it. Nor, sadly, will you be able to use any nice window-based interface, even if the host uses one: Telnet is a line-mode connection, so you're limited to text. You may get some limited graphics and colour, however, if your Telnet client has the right terminal emulations, and this is often one of the first questions an OPAC will ask you - what is your terminal type? The most basic emulation is dumb terminal or ttyy, which acts just as if you were printing out on a teletype printer. The most common type is probably VT100, which allows basic manipulation of the cursor on the screen, meaning you'll get selection boxes, menus etc. all working properly. Other types you'll commonly see are ANSI, VT220 and VT320. You should be able to get a basic working service out of any of these, but remember; the connection won't work unless your Telnet software and the host both choose the same emulation. If you log into another library's OPAC and the screens are a mess, you probably need to choose a different emulation as they don't match, and the mismatch is causing the gobbledegook.

So, it looks good, because we can get access to almost any major library in the world via Telnet. However, it also looks bad because we can so easily make mistakes with the addresses, logging in, configuring the terminal type etc. Wouldn't it be nice if there was a tool that worked like Telnet but which took care of all that awkward stuff for us?

Hytelnet

Well, fortunately, there is, and it's called Hytelnet. Hytelnet is short for hyper-Telnet, and it's an extension of Telnet which was developed at the University of

Saskatchewan. It makes Telnet connections just like an ordinary Telnet client, but it allows us to choose which ones to make by using a hyper-textual menu system. With Hytelnet you can easily build menu-like structures which can be used to re-member information about the nature of connections you make.

It gets better, as not only can you make your own lists which can be accessed in this way, saving you the bother of remembering what the address was for that particular library you wanted (rather like having a push-button call memory on your 'phone), but also you can use other peoples' lists and save yourself the bother of having to find out in the first place the addresses and logins for places you might want to visit. Conveniently, some sites have made a particular point of building Hytelnet links to other libraries. The best point of access has been from the Radcliffe Sci-ence Library at Oxford , which unfortunately has just withdrawn its public access to this service because of levels of demand - you now need a personal login to access it instead of just using "hytelnet" as a login. Other hytelnet-based systems where you can browse a geographically-organised list of many of the world's li-braries and select a connection which gives you all the information you need to get connected - even in foreign languages or on unusual systems - include web-based interfaces to hytelnet systems such as that based at Cambridge.

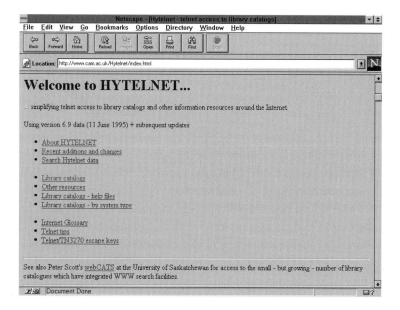

Figure 1: Accessing library OPACs using web-based Hytelnet at Cambridge

Data capture

This easy connection to other libraries' systems is all very well, but we also want to make use of the information we see. Sometimes we might be checking a location for an interlibrary loan request, or looking for a bibliographic record; we usually want to re-use part or all of the data which is flashed on the screen before us. We could simply write down the information, but that's terribly wasteful of time (since we often want to incorporate it back into a machine-readable document at the end of the day) and also makes it prone to error - long class numbers, for instance, can easily be miscopied. Also, we might want data from several different bits of the display, or different pages. Is there some way to keep a machine readable copy of the screens of information we see during a Telnet session?

The answer is yes, several ways. Firstly, most Telnet clients have some kind of "logging" facility which allows a straight copy of the data stream received to be kept in a file for future use. This sounds great, as it means all we see is kept. However, it's not quite as straightforward as it sounds if, for instance, you want to load the data into a wordprocessor and edit it. The data stream contains not only the text you see on the screen, but also (in most cases) additional coded information to, for example, move the cursor around the screen, or tab out parts of the data. Simply reading a log of such a stream into a wordprocessor results in lots of gobbledegook embedded around the text, instead of it being laid out as originally intended. You can edit such a log, but it's a lot of hard work. If your Telnet client supports "text-only" logging, this means the control characters are not stored, which makes things considerably easier; although you will almost certainly still need to do some tidying of the text data.

Windows-based Telnet clients can be particularly useful for data capture, as they usually have some kind of "scrollback" feature, which allows you to not only go back and look at what you've seen, but also to copy from the buffer to the Windows clipboard and then paste into a Windows wordprocessor. This is a particularly effective way to assemble a document from a number of different source elements - you simply copy them over as you go. Be aware if you use this feature, however, that these buffers have a limited size, and the oldest data gets pushed out of the buffer without warning to make space for new. So if you are planning a big session, either copy out what you need as you go, or set the buffer size big enough to hold the data you intend to view - it's user-configurable in most clients.

Key tips for the effective use of Telnet and Hytelnet

- Know the terminal emulation(s) your Telnet client is capable of and use the best available
- If the screen shows garbage, try a different terminal type
- If in doubt logging into a remote system, try the obvious name first
- As a guest user, if a password is required, try your email address
- Use Hytelnet to make Telnet access easier
- Use a good remote source to find lists of sites' addresses and login information
- Remember the instructions for logging off!
- Log online data you may need again
- Cut and paste in Windows for easy data capture
- Be aware of the size of your scrollback buffer and don't exceed it.

5. FTP and Archie

So far, we have looked at tools for passing messages and opening lines of communication with other computers. However, a large proportion of movement of data around the Internet relates to the identification and retrieval of *files* of some kind. Be it a thesis, a photograph, a set of figures, a press release or a computer program, all of these different data are stored on computers as files, so we need some mechanisms for identifying and retrieving files across the Internet. Among the oldest and most important of the Internet tool are FTP and Archie, which perform these functions.

FTP

FTP stands for File Transfer Protocol, and as its name implies, it is the fundamental method of transferring files of data around the Internet. Before the development of some of the more user-friendly tools such as Gopher and the WWW, FTP was the key method by which data was exchanged. Built on the client-server model, FTP appears to users rather like a mini-environment, with its own command-line prompt and arcane set of commands. First, you connect to a remote site by giving your client the address of its FTP server, very much as you would make a Telnet connection. Next you must log on to the host server. The norm for this procedure, unless you are accessing a computer on which you hold a personal account, is to use the login name "anonymous" (which is why you often hear this referred to as "Anonymous FTP"). You will probably also be asked for a password, where again there is a norm; you simply type in your email address (in full: *id@sitename*, not just your id or site). Not every system requires this, but many will not accept your login unless you supply a valid email address. Consider it a courtesy to the organisations who are granting you the rights to saunter through their machines to let them know who you are! Then you navigate down through the directory structure of the host computer (strangely enough, often using commands which look like DOS commands even though you're normally talking to a UNIX computer) until you reach the place where the file you want is kept, and then you tell the client to retrieve it. You can also send files to a remote host (uploading) as well as retrieving them (downloading).

There is one particularly important idiosyncrasy to the system, which can result in your efforts retrieving nothing more than gobbledegook if you're not aware of it. FTP distinguishes between ASCII data (plain text files) and other binary files, and transfers each of them in a different fashion. If you haven't told FTP to use the right format for the data you want, it still downloads, but will garble the contents. Worse, it's not always possible to be sure whether a file is ASCII or not - although you can normally make a good guess. ASCII files usually have the extension .txt, or no extension at all. Anything with an executable extension (.com, .exe), a compression system extension (.zip, .arc, .tar, and quite a few others), or a binary data extension (lots!) is a binary file. Don't forget that word processed documents are also binary documents, not ASCII, because they have a lot of embedded codes relating to their formatting inside them, so .doc files are binary files too! If you do download something and it turns out to be rubbish, try again with the other format.

A less important but extremely irritating idiosyncrasy is that FTP doesn't tell you anything about the status of a transfer request until it finishes - unless you ask it to at the outset. Before you start a download, type "hash" at the FTP command prompt to get a visual indication of how far the transfer has got. This normally prints one hash sign on the screen for each 1k of data transferred, and allows you to judge whether or not it's worth continuing, or breaking off and trying again later. You should also remember to rename files with names of more than eight characters which you are downloading from a UNIX system to a DOS one, as otherwise DOS will simply truncate the filename. This can be rather frustrating if you're downloading more than one file with similar names, as one may overwrite another! The download command in FTP is "get *filename*"; to change the name of the received file to be different from the original simply add a third parameter with the new name ("get *filename newname*").

If all of this sounds complicated, you can be glad that Windows-based FTP clients are now very common which makes things rather easier in some respects, as they typically use normal Windows dialogue boxes, one to represent your machine's directories and files, and one for the remote host. All you need to do is navigate up and down the directory structure at each end to find the file you want and where you want to put it, and then hit the transfer or copy button to start the process. This does make it easier to browse for related items and to check for errors. Some even have automatic file type detection, although others still require you to identify the file type and set it appropriately, and still always give you a visual indication of the state of the transfer.

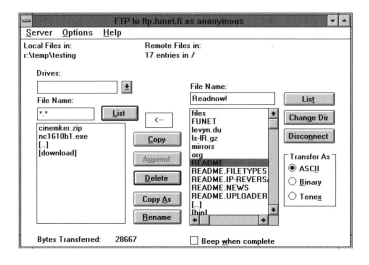

Figure 2: An FTP transfer using WinFTP

Archie

The biggest question of all in this - how do we find out where the files we want are? A partial answer to this question comes in the form of Archie.

Archie is the oldest of the mass search tools on the Internet, and can be an extremely useful one in the right circumstances. For information professionals, though, it is critical that we understand the limitations of Archie, if we are not to waste a lot of time and become very frustrated with its apparent inability to find what we want.

Archie servers are quite limited in number by comparison with other resources: around the world, they are numbered in tens rather than hundreds or thousands. However, the majority of them have a very wide geographical scope, collecting and indexing available files on an international basis (although some are restricted primarily to a country or even region within a country). They work by sending messages to all the FTP sites they know about on a regular basis, asking for information about what files they have available. The data these sites return is then compiled into an index which is what is searched when we contact them. But what exactly is this data?

The problem is that the only information Archie normally records and indexes are the names and locations of the files available for transfer, so this is all we can search. We cannot look at the content of the files, or any description or conceptual indexing of them - only their filenames. And although we can use truncation and substitution searching, there are no Boolean or other relational operators in Archie - you supply single terms only. This means that for nearly all intents and purposes, we cannot do subject searching with Archie. Why? Take a look at the average directory listing. For the most part, even with long UNIX filenames, the names of the files are only vague approximations of content, often abbreviated, with different separators and so on. It's impossible to meaningfully name files for searching. How many times have you saved a file, only to forget its name and have difficulty retrieving *it on your own local system*? Now multiply that problem a millionfold and you begin to see why you can't find things on Archie with a "normal" subject searching approach.

You can only really use Archie effectively if, paradoxically, you already know what you're looking for. It is really more of a file locator than a search tool in the sense that information people typically conceive it. This is not as redundant as it might seem, however, for there are many times that finding the location of a file is just what you want to do; and also, with a little lateral thinking, you can sometimes use Archie to help you track down resources you might be interested in, even if you can't get it to take you straight to them.

A typical use of Archie might be to find a convenient local site for a file you have seen mentioned somewhere else. Getting data from busy FTP sites across the Atlantic can be an extremely tedious affair; if you can find a local site for the file, it can often be quicker to do an Archie search and retrieve from that local site than to try to get it from across the pond. And many files are duplicated across many locations. If you're trying to get a paper from an individual, it *may* only be available for one site, but if it's anything useful which is released into the public domain, the chances are that there are many copies of it about. PD and shareware programs for instance, are available from many software archives throughout the world, so if you are looking for an HTML editor to help you with your web documents for instance (see later!) or some FAQ (Frequently Asked Questions) or RFC (Request For Comment) files on a subject, these are likely to be widely available.

31

But what if you *don't* know the name of the file you want? How can we use Archie to help us find information then? One thing we can do (and it's not as silly as it sounds) is to *guess* the name of the file we might want. For instance, using our HTML editor example, we might be looking for a copy of HTML Assistant for Windows. What might it be called? It can only be eight characters if it's a DOS/Windows file name; and sure enough, a search for HTMLA*.* will find the file we want. Or we could use a slightly different approach, which is as close as we can approximate subject searching with Archie.

As we said, the Archie index is mainly compiled simply of *filenames*. but of course, these files are stored in directories, each of which has a name, and each of which is stored in its parents' directory as - another filename! It's identified as a directory, but it's still there in the structure, and is indexed and can be found using Archie. This allows us to try searches for locations of groups of items which might be of interest by guessing the name of the directory we might expect to find such files in. It is far from foolproof, and as we shall see, there are usually better ways of searching for data, but if we're stuck, then searching for editors, or HTML, might turn up some good possibilities. Be aware of the false drop possibilities however: "editors" would also find regular text editors in abundance, for instance.

Although Archie is another client/server system, you normally Telnet to Archie sites and log in as Archie, using client software at the host site. You may have Archie client software available locally, however, which will allow you to prepare your search locally before connection; and it may also be available through another tool such as a WWW browser (e.g. ArchiePlexForm - see the WWW chapter). You can also typically do Archie searches by email in a similar manner to searching mail archives, as described in the previous chapter.

Key tips for the most effective use of FTP and Archie:

- For FTP, login as anonymous and give your email address as a password
- Use the # command to get information on the status of transfers
- Make sure you are using the correct mode for the files you are downloading
- If a file is corrupted, try again with the other mode
- Remember to rename long filenames going to a DOS system
- Different Archies will use different sources - be prepared to try more than one

- Don't expect Archie to perform effectively as a subject search tool
- Try guessing filenames (or their roots) if you don't know them
- Try to find directories which might contain what you're really looking for
- Use local resources first if possible.

6. Gopher and Veronica

Gopher

One of the first tools which really made a big difference to information provision and retrieval on the Internet was Gopher. Developed at the University of Minnesota, it is a "resource browser", a menu-based system for allowing information providers to very easily make their existing files of information accessible across the net, and to provide the Internet user with a simple interface with which they can browse what is available and retrieve anything they like the look of without having to deal with lots of arcane information and commands such as are needed to retrieve files with FTP. Today, Gopher has been largely superseded by the WWW, but there are still a few useful (if increasingly vestigial) Gopher resources out there.

How Gopher works

Gopher is another client-server based system which holds documents of two primary sorts, actual documents (which you might think of as primary data) and lists of references to such documents (which you might think of as secondary data). These "lists" hold the data needed by a Gopher client to recreate the menus which are used as an interface in this system; they are almost like "select bibliographies" compiled by the owners of the menu pages. The Gopher client receives the data for these menus and manipulates them into the useable form which you are presented with on screen, allows you to make choices from the items displayed, and takes care of relaying requests to the appropriate hosts in the appropriate format to get whatever you ask for, be it another menu, a text document, or some other sort of file.

Gophers exist for both line mode and GUI interfaces, which work in essentially the same ways. Additionally, web browsers are normally configured to be able to read Gopher resources, so you can use these as Gopher clients too.

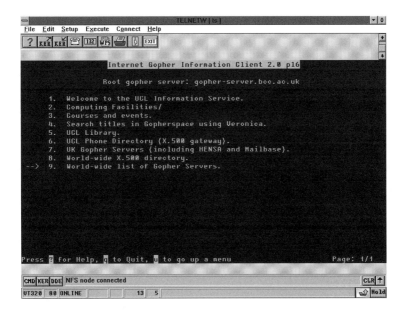

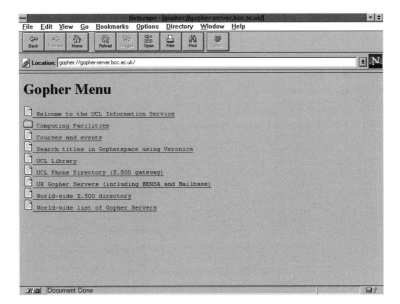

Figure 3: Line and graphic gopher interfaces

Data available are presented in the form of a menu, from which any item can be selected. Behind each line of description lies a "pointer" to the location of the source material, which includes some simple information on the nature of the data as well as its location. When an item is selected, the client sends a request to the appropriate host and, on receipt, displays it for you.

There are two points to note here. Firstly, when you look at a Gopher menu retrieved from a particular site, you should be aware that the entries in the menu could be located *anywhere* on the Internet, not necessarily at the same site you have received the menu from. Unfortunately most gophers don't give you any immediate idea of where an item on a menu comes from - or of how big an item is. This can be a major problem if, for instance, you start to download a big file from the USA to the UK in mid-afternoon! You can break a slow transmission, but if you don't know how long you've still got to go, it's a stressful business - will it finish if I give it another minute? Perhaps it's only got a few kilobytes to go...

Secondly, most gophers do not actually display the contents of non-menu documents themselves but call other programs to do it, thus enabling them to potentially handle a very wide range of materials. Telnet and FTP connections can be made via Gopher, and text and image viewers of many types can also be configured. The important point is that, unless your particular client has a suitable viewer configured to deal with the type of data you have requested, it will give you an error - and, even more frustratingly, only after it has loaded the data, which it then discards! One classic example is that Hgopher (a common Windows-based gopher client) comes configured to use the Windows Notepad as its text viewer. Unfortunately, Notepad can only deal with files up to a certain size, so when you have patiently waited for your 100k document to download, you will get a polite message saying that it's too large for Notepad, and be presented with a blank screen. Your only options in such a case are to configure a different viewer, or to download the document again to a file. Many people are unaware of the download facility within Gopher, but it can be very useful for such circumstances. From a line mode Gopher client, shift-D invokes the download procedure; from a Windows client, there is usually a button to click to switch from view mode (an eye) to download mode (a folder).

As we have seen, data is organised within the Gopher system as menus. Typically, when we use Gopher, we call up a menu (our home system's Gopher server top level menu is the normal starting place) and follow from one link in broadly a hierarchical fashion, until we find something useful or interesting. Gopher menus make exploring the Internet an easy task. But if we have navigated through a dozen menus to find something we like, can we remember how we got there? And do we want to go through the same convoluted route to get there next time? Of course not. Gopher provides us with an incredibly useful facility, which we will find has been copied by other systems such as the WWW, to keep track of useful places and resources we find. This is what is known as *bookmarking*.

Bookmarks

Bookmarks work by recording the pointer information which lies behind the Gopher menu entries. After all, there is no fixed link between one menu and another piece of data - as we said, you can link to anywhere from a single menu page. The nicest thing about bookmarks on Gopher is that, being composed of Gopher menu entry data, they can be displayed to you as another personalised Gopher menu. So, when you look at your bookmarks, you look at a Gopher menu, and you can jump straight to the entries you have previously found and marked by simply selecting the item. Gopher clients don't usually give you any tools for doing anything other than adding to your personal bookmark list, but since the data is only ASCII text, it is a simple matter to edit your bookmarks in any word processor. Be careful though; if you do edit your bookmark file, you must save it as an ASCII text file, and not as a wordprocessor document, otherwise your Gopher client will not recognise it. This is because wordprocessors normally embed a lot of coded information (about format and layout, for example) in their files.

By creating a personal bookmark list, you can build a tremendously useful resource for future use. It is very hard to just come to the Internet and use it as a reference tool, but it is perfectly feasible to construct a useful reference set of locations over time with bookmarks, and this is one of the most important keys to making efficient use of the Internet for information work.

Subject trees

So far so good, but short of simply hunting for link after link, how do we find information on a Gopher? One simple method, and a very good starting point for general subject-based enquiries, is to use Gopher *subject trees*. Subject trees are not unique to the Gopher system, of course; but they lend themselves very well to the Gopher environment, and many originated on Gopher servers.

As information workers, we should all be familiar with the concept of a subject tree - any hierarchical classification system works on this principle. Starting with broad concepts, we can follow a path down progressively more precise descriptions until we come to what we want. It is easy to see how this method of organising and searching for data is a natural candidate for a system like Gopher consisting of menus within menus. One of the best trees to use as a starting point is that of BUBL's (the Bulletin Board for Libraries) LINK, which originated as a gopher subject tree, although it is now available as a web-based system browseable by alphabetic subject categories or by Dewey classification, or free-text searcheable (see resource guide in the appendix).

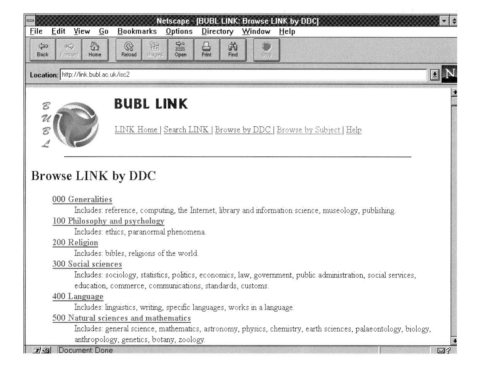

Figure 4: Part of the BUBL LINK subject tree

Nearly every major server has a subject tree. Many items on a given tree may also appear on other trees - others may be unique. Always remember that any one subject tree is simply one person's (or a group of people's) view of the best resources - not necessarily the only or the best view. Especially if you want to be exhaustive, don't rely on a single tree. If you constantly find references to the same sources on different trees, this is usually a good indication as to the quality of a site. And don't forget; note the good sources down as bookmarks. You can start to build your own subject tree this way!

However, using the subject tree approach can be very long-winded, particularly on a Gopher system (we will talk about web-based trees later) - and especially if the information you are looking for is fairly specific. If this is the case, and you are using a Gopher resource, there is a search tool called Veronica which can be called upon.

Veronica

Veronica is used to search Gopher menus for keywords. When you perform a search using Veronica, the results are presented as another Gopher menu which you can then use to jump to any of the resources found, just like any other Gopher menu.

Veronica servers actually create a keyword index from the words used to describe the entries on Gopher menus. They use as their database not only their own system's Gopher resources, but also the resources of other Gopher servers they know about. Thus if you search using a Veronica server at, say, Manchester, you are also simultaneously searching the records of many other UK sites (and a lot of overseas sites too). The results you get from using one Veronica server may well differ from another, as it will have looked at a different selection of systems to compile its index. Unfortunately, there is no way to easily find out what systems the Veronica you are using has actually looked at, although this is not usually a problem, as the "what " is more important than the "where"! So once again, it can be worth trying different servers in different locations if you want to be exhaustive in your searching. And although Veronica, like Gopher, is rather out of fashion, you may be suprised at the number of Veronica servers that are still out there.

Searching with Veronica

There are usually two options for Veronica searches. One allows you to search for any Gopher entry, i.e. document titles and directory titles, whilst the other restricts your search to entries which refer to directories only. Whichever you choose, you will be presented with a dialogue box asking you for the words you want to search for. But why would you want to differentiate between the two?

Let us retrace our steps for a moment, and think about some of the likely outcomes of searching using a tool like Veronica. We have said, the entries in a Veronica index are the words used in the Gopher menus to describe items. That means an item's description is limited to some half-a-dozen words. Although Veronica allows us to use complex Boolean searching, it really isn't very profitable to do so, because the size of the target is so small. If you find a match for your six-term search statement, it will doubtless be a very good match - but your recall ratio will be very, very poor. It is vital to remember that when you use Veronica, you are free-text searching the menu entries for, *not the contents of*, the documents concerned. But perhaps the most important point to consider, and the reason for most failed searches using Veronica, is the way in which items are organised in gopher menus, and the ramifications that has for the descriptions we are searching.

Gopher is inherently hierarchical, and subject information on Gopher very naturally tends to be organised in that fashion - as we discussed when talking about subject trees. What this means for the description of items on Gopher servers is that often, important conceptual information about the content of a given resource is contained not only in the description of the item itself, but is also *implicit in the location* of the item within the menu hierarchy. When we search using Veronica, we can access only the information in the description, not in the locational context. This means that we will often fail to find perfectly valuable pieces of information because key concepts are missing from the descriptions we are searching.

To give a simple example: imagine we want to find information on roman archaeology in England. We have three well-defined concepts here: a time period (roman), a field of endeavour (archaeology) and a geographical location (England). It would seem natural to put a simple search together thus: Roman and archaeolog* and (England or UK or Britain) - syntactically, a perfectly acceptable veronica query. You might think we've covered the requirements - and so we have in logical terms. We may indeed get some hits - but we may not. The question we must ask ourselves is, what is the likelihood of items on this subject being so completely described, as menu entries, in the *context* of where they are likely to be found? More than likely, such data will have already been conceptually subdivided, so the descriptions will NOT contain all these terms. The reality might be that the data is in an entry entitled "Archaeology" in a menu titled "Roman Britain", or vice versa, or just titled "Roman archaeological sites" on a gopher of British tourist attractions!

Thus it can be seen that Veronica searching can be a rather hit-or-miss affair. If you have a concept which is unified and singular, for instance a name of a person or place or event, Veronica can be a very good way to find it quickly. If the requirement is clearly subject-based, you may be better off searching via a subject tree. But you could also try thinking a little laterally, and ask yourself: "What might the menu be called where I could find an item containing this data?" You can then search for *directory entries only* (i.e. menu titles) in Veronica, and find sources *within which* you can look for your required information. With a little practice in this way of thinking, you can get quite effective results!

Other considerations

A few final considerations on the use of Veronica. If you bookmark the results of a veronica search, the information that is actually saved is not the *outcome* of your search, but the *request*. If you subsequently pick such a bookmark, your old search statement will be automatically dispatched to wherever you sent it before for *re-processing*, and you will get a bang-up-to-date list of items matching your search. If you have a suitable search statement, this can be very useful as a current awareness aid, as by comparing the old list to the new one you can quickly see what new resources have become available.

Another problem you can encounter is that of large numbers of identically-named items in your search results. The problem here is in knowing whether they are different resources with the same name, or simply repetitions of pointers to the same resource. As we mentioned, the way in which Veronica builds its indexes (by going round to different sites and examining the Gopher menus there) combined with the popularity of good sites (resulting in many other menus having pointers to them) means that the latter case is often true; these are pointers which have been taken from different locations, but which all point to the same place. Unfortunately, there is no convenient de-duplication system in any of the Gopher clients I know of at time of writing (although it shouldn't be that difficult to write one - somebody?) but at least you don't have to check by actually calling up each item. The info key ("=", or the item icon in windows-based systems) will show you, amongst other things, the pointer to the resource in question. If two entries' pointers are identical, it's the same resource. This also goes for items with different names, as the description isn't immutably linked to the pointer. So you need to do some checking before you really know if you've got 50 items, or just 50 references to the same item.

The problem of high levels of redundant entries in veronica searches isn't only with repetition - it's also with irrelevant data. Perhaps the biggest single difficulty in this area is that of course unit information. A typical search for a generalised subject in veronica will almost always bring up at least a sprinkling (if not a deluge) of strange entries with mystic strings of numbers and letters attached.

41

Call up one of these and you are likely to get a handful of lines giving you a room number, time and perhaps a few other short pieces of information about a course being run somewhere on the subject you're interested in. In most cases, this will be of no interest to you (and, sadly, even if you are looking for courses, these entries usually don't tell you the institution they're being held at - another example of the contextually implicit location problem we mentioned earlier) as they come from college and university CWIS, and have been provided to help local students plan their modular courses! Fortunately, because of the inclusion of the course codes in the gopher descriptions(for that's what those strange strings are) they can at least be quite easily recognised as such and time not wasted on them.

Lastly, before you start searching, it is a good idea to read some of the documents about using Veronica which you will commonly find on the same gopher menus as the search tool itself, such as how to compose queries, or about common questions and answers (FAQ files). It can be helpful to print these off for reference, as they contain a lot of useful details, tips and hints.

Key tips for the effective use of Gopher and Veronica:

- If you find a good source - bookmark it!
- Build up your bookmark collection for use as a ready reference source
- Use subject trees as a starting point for general subject-based enquiries
- Create multiple bookmark files for different subject areas - a personal subject tree
- Use Veronica for more specific enquiries, especially unified conceptual descriptions
- Bookmark Veronica searches for a simple current awareness aid
- Don't normally use more than a couple of terms in a Veronica search
- If a Veronica search isn't working, try looking for a menu using a broader term
- Check the descriptions of items with "=" or the item icon to find where they're held
- Download items you can't immediately use with the "D" key or folder icon
- If you get stuck, get online help with "?", "h" or the help menu in Windows clients
- Don't forget you can use WWW clients for Gopher browsing.

7.WAIS

WAIS stands for Wide Area Information Server, and is yet another client-server based method of information browsing and retrieval. Amongst the many information retrieval tools on the Internet, WAIS is unusual in that it actually fits the information professional's usual conceptual model of an information retrieval system, bearing some considerable analogy to traditional online searching in its structure and techniques (although, as ever, it has some particular problems). It is another rapidly-growing resource, and one which many information people should quickly feel at home with.

WAIS grew from a business concept originally developed by Apple, Thinking Machines and Dow Jones for a tool which would allow access to and retrieval from many different datasets on a paying basis. Small wonder then, perhaps, that it follows more closely than any other net tool the model of retrieval from a traditional online host. The concept is a simple one; first choose the data sets you want to search in, so that you only look where you think the information will be, then search within those sources. This two-stage search pattern is of course exactly like the familiar one of traditional online searching where we select some appropriate databases on a host, and then search in those databases only.

What actually happens when you work with WAIS is that you select your sources from a list held by the WAIS system, give it your search instructions, and then the client actually contacts other servers (the ones on which your selected resources reside) and gets them to run the searches, collecting the results from these different requests and finally passing them back to you.

The key thing about WAIS is that it is designed to access indexed data, usually full-text free-text-indexed data. So unlike the tools we have looked at so far, WAIS actually selects documents on the basis of their true contents, and not just an overly brief and simplistic description of the item. Thus, finally, here we have a tool which actually fits our expectations and experience of electronic searching more accurately. LIS workers should have no trouble getting to grips with this aspect of the way WAIS works.

43

When you start a WAIS client, either locally or by connecting to a public WAIS location, the first thing you see is a screen showing the resource bases the client knows about.

From here you select the resources you wish to search (usually with the space bar). If you are using a starting point with many resources, you can search for the ones you want by using the "/" key followed by the name you're looking for. You can select more than one resource from the list. Apart from the immediate resources you see, you can often find directories of servers (the classic one is at quake.think.com and is called directory-of-servers) to search to find more sources to investigate.

Once you have selected the resources you want to search, call up the dialogue box to enter your actual search terms (usually with the "w" key). The strategy you enter here is the one passed to the servers whose resources you have identified, and the results are returned to you as a further menu. Some WAIS systems accept simple Boolean logic and truncation (usually with the "*"), so more complex search strategies are possible, but the system also works on a ranked searching basis, so that if you enter a series of terms, the system will try to match any or all of them, and first return the items which have the most occurrences of the most words. From here, you can select the specific documents you are interested in and either view them or mail them to yourself. When viewing the data, the keywords you used are highlighted in the text. Some WAIS systems also incorporate a relevance feedback system which allow you to effectively search for more on the basis of items you have already found which you like.

Although it seems that WAIS should be an ideal system for us, it's still not problem-free. Despite its basic common format (originally based around the then-developing Z39.50 standard for the exchange of information) different sites operate in subtly different ways which can be confusing to the end-user. In particular, if you do not have a local client for your system, trying to actually get hold of the resources you want to search can sometimes be very difficult.

A further problem is that creating records for WAIS resources can be far more time-consuming than, for instance, preparing a gopher entry, and thus many sites don't bother to use WAIS to index their resources. This relative shortage of material combined with the difficulty you can experience in accessing sources not locally indexed can make searching with WAIS a frustrating experience on occasion as you fail to find data you expect to be out there. Sadly, in my view, WAIS has become something of a missed opportunity: more and more sites are actually using WAIS as a means of providing local full-text search access to their resources, but virtually none are orienting this facility towards its originally intended use of easy wider access. Could we see something similar happening with Z39.50, one might ask? I think the answer is probably yes (but then that's a different book...).

Key tips for the effective use of WAIS:

- Try to use a local client if you can to gain better control over your resource lists
- Beware of subtle differences in implementation between public sites
- If limited to public sites, "shop around" for one you like
- Use directories of servers to identify which resources to search
- Discriminate in your resource selection for the most focused results
- Where available, use relevance feedback to improve selection
- Use the mail facility to send yourself copies of documents you find.

8. The World Wide Web

The World Wide Web (or WWW, or W3, or simply, the web) is the fastest-growing, highest-profile part of the Internet today. Some have argued that it was largely because of the development of the WWW that we saw the enormous growth in the Internet which took place from the early 90s, which although in my view may be an overstatement, does have some truth in it. What cannot be argued against is that it has become, a major factor in Internet development, and the vehicle of choice for many information providers and consumers.

What is it?

The WWW is yet another client/server based system to allow easy access to distributed resources. Like the other systems we have looked at, it is oriented around the use of links, pointers from the resource or document you might have in front of you to others elsewhere on different systems. But where it differs from any other current tools on the Internet, is that it is a *hypermedia* system. Hypermedia is a combination of hypertext and multimedia, the former a child of the computing age, the latter one which has been with us for a while but which is increasingly used in the computing context. Hypertext is text which can be accessed in a non-linear fashion, according to the user's needs or whim. A hypertext document is organised as a number of pages, each of which have parts of the text which act as pointers to other pages in the document. If users want to know more about one of these linked elements, they simply select it and are presented with the relevant page, which in turn contains both ordinary and linked text, from which they can proceed down a new path, or return to the previous page (or their starting point) to take a different track. Multimedia is of course something which involves more than one of the traditional media in combination, most typically sound and visual data of either the static or moving variety, although today's web browsers can be configured to deal with almost any form of material your machine can physically support. Hypermedia is thus a combination of the hypertextual navigation system of links within documents/pages with additional non-textual forms of data: a form of media which is naturally suited to exploit the capabilities of modern-day desktop computing.

How does it work?

The primary motive force behind the WWW is a thing called Hypertext Mark-up Language (HTML). To build a basic web page, you start with the text you want to use (along with files for any other media you want included - an image file containing a logo, for instance) in simple, ASCII format. Then you *mark up* the page with *HTML tags* which provide instructions about what the various bits of the text are - headings, titles, lists, pictures to be displayed, and (most importantly) links to other web pages or resources. You can include instructions to display fill-in forms, emphasise text, draw lines on the screen and many other operations, simply by adding ASCII text tags (enclosed in angle brackets) which define what is to be done with the data which follows them. Your pages are then stored on a server, and the WWW client software, when it retrieves a web page, reads the HTML tags and interprets them, processing and displaying the different parts of the document accordingly.

Inherent strengths and weaknesses of WWW

There are a number of important strengths of the WWW as an information delivery system - but there are also some considerable weaknesses, which I believe are far too often glossed over in the media love affair with the web. And paradoxically, what is an advantage in one way can be a disadvantage in another. Perhaps the most obvious example of this is the graphic and multimedia capability of the web.

Probably the biggest single reason that the WWW has become so popular, particularly with the media, is that its ability to include and display graphics makes it *look pretty* by comparison with its text-based Internet predecessors. Pages packed with art, colour, cartoons, icons, animations and the like are immensely more eye-catching than a page of plain text, and the ability to project more powerful visual layouts have been one of the major draws for the commercial world to become interested in the web as a means of disseminating information and advertising. After all, who is drawn to an advert in plain text over rather than a pretty pictorial representation? Very few. And it would be difficult to argue that a well-illustrated page was not more effective in transferring information than a purely textual one.

But there are a number of other considerations here. Remember the old saying, a picture is worth a thousand words? A well-chosen, apposite picture may well be, but many web page authors still splatter images around just for the sake of prettification, rather than to genuinely assist in getting information across. And we should consider not only the worth of a picture, but also its cost; which in Internet terms is more likely to be an order of magnitude greater than the saying would have us believe. To retrieve and display a screenful of text requires the transmission of typically a mere one or two thousand bytes of information. To retrieve and display a full-screen image of high quality can easily require the transmission of several *hundred* thousand bytes of data, and of course, this transmission takes time. Even with careful processing and data compression, any page containing graphics takes *many* times longer to download than such a page without graphics, and can often result in long waits for the user. Worse, the biggest single problem faced by users today is network congestion, caused by too much data trying to travel through too little bandwidth; and thus not only do all these graphics take longer per se to download, they also help to create an even bigger data jam on the laughably-named information superhighway, which increasingly resembles the busier portions of the UK's M25 at rush-hour, complete with identical frustrations as we sit waiting for something to happen whilst nothing moves. Fortunately, most browsers come with an option to turn images off, and (to be fair) some producers are becoming more responsible in trying to keep graphical content to a positively-selected minimum. But the explosion of graphical traffic on the Internet has been, and continues to be, a major inconvenience and frustration to the transfer of information across it. The web is a godsend to sites which truly need multimedia ability, such as galleries and museums, but for ordinary information provision, the multimedia capability of the WWW is far more likely to be abused than capitalised upon.

Another double-edged sword is the richness of data in web pages. As each page comprises of not only links but also much text which describes the document, it is a relatively simple matter to gather that text into a full-text index, making such a page eminently more retrievable by conventional means than could ever be the case with the limited (or non-existent) descriptions provided in the most of the other systems we have looked at. However, this increased quality of description comes at the cost of indexing effort which is again much greater than that applied in most other systems. This in turn means that comprehensive indexes of web resources require massive computing resources to assemble. The free, originally academically-sponsored web search services of the early days of the web have almost entirely become commercial ventures now, supported by advertising revenue (and generating more network congestion as a result of the interminable adverts they have to carry!) in a bid to support the ever-increasing costs of more people searching more data. However even these monster sites are suffering from a range of problems in trying to satisfy the insatiable hunger of the net community for reliable ways of finding the information they want. I think these problems will inevitably lead to a conceptual change in our approach to most information retrieval from the Internet, and which already shows signs of happening (see the final chapter for more on this).

And as we have said, web data is the fastest area of growth on the Internet, due to a combination of its visual appeal and the ease with which anyone can set themselves up as a "web publisher". This too compounds the above problem, and also helps to create another - that of quality control. As every student, personal subscriber and attention-seeker on the net creates web pages reflecting their interests, the volume swells inestimably but the quality (in most cases) suffers greatly. How do we, as potential consumers of such information that people promulgate on their pages, know whether it is accurate or inaccurate, true or false, good data or poor data? Although there may be an implication of quality associated with information provided by certain sites or corporate providers, this is no guarantee, and of course the most interesting data gleaned from the unprovenanced pages of enthusiastic individuals who make up the majority of web page provision can only be used at your peril - whether you pay or not! This is not to say, of course, that all information from "enthusiastic individuals" is of poor quality or unreliable - on the contrary, some of the very best specialist information resources on the net come from exactly this quarter. The point, and the problem, is that we usually have no method of differentiating the good from the bad on the web other than by our own judgement, which in such cases must often be extremely arbitrary.

Despite the rush of commercial enterprises to the Internet as a means of reaching a well-off and technically able audience, there is a dearth of free, hard, commercially-related information on the Internet. Certain public data can be had, such as some census and filing data, but for the most part, company information, marketing information and the like is extremely scarce on the open net. No wonder, in one sense, as almost by definition this data is valuable, and therefore those who collate it wish to sell it rather than give it away. It is certainly possible to locate sources of such data operating on the Internet, but the great majority of them require your registration and your money before they part with useful data. The only "free" commercial sources tend to be those *advertising* services, not providing data.

If this all sounds very "doom and gloom", don't be put off - the web can be an excellent source of material, and retrieval from it easier than any other Internet source. It is simply that, as I said at the outset, we as information professionals need to have an honest view of the various Internet tools, which means recognising and allowing for the weaknesses in the system. If we expect the WWW to be a panacea, we will be sorely disappointed. If we recognise its shortcomings and capitalise on its strengths, however, we will have another highly useful resource to add to our armoury.

Browsers

Unlike most of the other Internet tools, who have only a few clients to choose from, the WWW has spawned a considerable number of clients, normally referred to as browsers. All of them perform with a common basic functionality, but each in a subtly different way. Some even go beyond the current standards of HTML, providing extensions which can do things ordinary HTML can't, and almost all allow the use of add-in applications, extra programs which can perform functions and deal with data outside the scope of normal HTML. Here we shall consider the common features of the mainstream browsers and the best ways to use them.

First and foremost, all web browsers support the use of bookmarks, as Gopher does. Most of the major ones, such as Netscape, provide not only the ability to save bookmarks of valuable sites, but also to edit those lists, even to the extent of categorising them into hierarchies as they grow larger. As with gopher, the importance of building and maintaining a good, personal bookmark file cannot be understated.

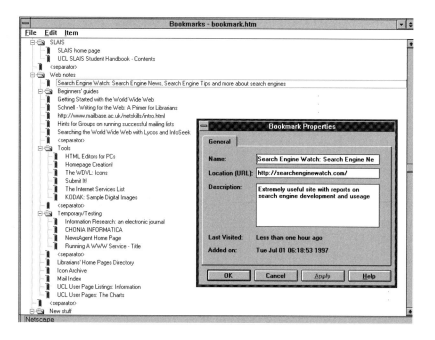

Figure 5: Bookmark organisation in Netscape

Most modern browsers have inbuilt capability to handle common, simple data types, but all also have the ability to call other client programs to handle data of specific natures. This is done very simply by linking the file extensions of retrieved data to specific applications programs, so that if data arrives in one form, it is passed to an appropriate application to display or use it. This makes web browsers very flexible as they can be quickly reconfigured to take advantage of changes and developments in other applications software.

This capability to handle data types also extends to the ability to access other tools' data. This means that it is not necessary to have a separate gopher client, or even a newsreader: modern web browsers can handle all these data types seamlessly. A web browser can happily access a gopher server, retrieve and display a gopher menu, connect to a news server and read and answer articles from a newsgroup, or talk to WAIS and Archie servers and get data from them. Perhaps the biggest benefit here is the convenience in not having to switch systems, and the encouragement it gives to data providers to incorporate links to all types of resources from the web.

Despite its graphic capability, it is recognised that not all users are able to access web resources through a graphic link. There also exist non-graphic web browsers, such as Lynx, which can work with web resources through a line-based interface only, downloading non-text resources as files where required and presenting pages through a purely hypertextual interface.

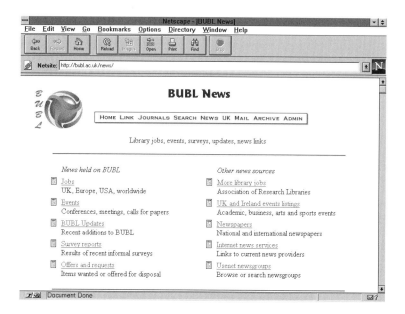

Figure 6: Web data seen from Netscape

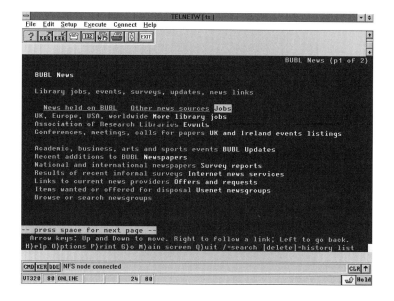

Figure 7: Web data seen from Lynx

All browsers allow the capture of the data which makes up a web page, or the *source*. This usually takes the form of a "save file" option, which copies the source data for the page to a local disk. This can be a very useful way of keeping data in a more accessible form (for instance to save the time of repeatedly downloading a large page across the Atlantic) but can have some unexpected drawbacks pertaining to links from the document. Web references, just like pathnames in any operating system, can be either *relative* or *absolute*. Absolute references are the sort you see in the press: they look something like: http://www.ucl.ac.uk/SLAIS/slais.htm

This is the URL (Uniform Resource Locator) for UCL's Library School's home page and is what you would see as a location on the screen if you tried to access it. However, within a given page, further links from it may be absolute (i.e. the full URL, as above) or relative, that is to say simply the location of the new data in relation to the source of the current page. Within the example above, there are links to the various other pages of the school's site: within the document they are entered simply as stafflst.htm (etc.). The browser knows, when it sees such a reference, to add the current "path" to the link name - just as an operating system assumes the current directory to be the location of a requested file unless you tell it otherwise. The problem here is that, if you save a copy of the file locally and subsequently call it up, the "source" of the page is your local system, not its original source, and so a relative link call will try to find the next page on your local disk, not where it actually is, resulting in an error message.

Why do people use these relative references? Because it actually makes it easier to keep control of multi-page documents that way. If you renamed or changed the location of the files, using absolute references, you'd have to re-edit every single document. With relative links, you can move them all without having to change any link except the first one. Also, it effectively forces people to "come in by the front door", to enter your document at the point you want , which makes keeping statistical data about usage that much easier. It is of course possible as a user to either edit the references in your local copy of the file, or also download the source for the links to get around this - but that's seldom worth the time involved. The main thing is to be aware that this can happen, and to know the way around it if need be.

From a web page producer's point of view, a common fallacy is that users will see a web page as they intended it. This is not necessarily true. Although the situation is changing with the introduction of alternative standards such as Adobe's PDF for the definition of pages, HTML still doesn't *define* a document in the layout sense you might expect. Its tags still are primarily structural, functional tags, and even if you now specify the absolute font, for instance, of a particular piece of text, it may not be acted upon by the browser at the client's end. What defines the final appearance of any web page on any browser is the set-up of that browser and system locally, for the user can specify some aspects of how the HTML tags are to be interpreted. Although newer developments such as Cascading Style Sheets (CSS) and dynamic markup do give considerably more control over such elements than was previously the case - at the expense of not being universally implemented - they still do not give guaranteed control over appearance. So if a document you are viewing seems to have funny line lengths, layouts or alignments when you view it, try changing your window size or font settings (usually in a preferences or options menu somewhere, depending on your browser).

Another of the key things about a hypermedia document is supposed to be that users can create their own ways through the document, jumping around as items take their fancy; that it is *non-linear* whereas traditional texts are linear (i.e. read page by page in a strict, predetermined order). I say supposed to be as I think ordinary texts too can be used in a non-linear fashion - haven't you ever jumped to a chapter or page in a book after consulting an index or contents page? - but perhaps that argument really belongs in a different book. An appreciation of structure is very important to most users if they are to effectively use hypermedia resources - we like to know where we are, where we're going, and what the possibilities or choices are. Good hypermedia resources try to provide this by clear identification of pages, links to important structural nodes (such as the starting page of the document and any important subgenus or branching points). But of course these are considerations primarily for page designers, rather than users. At least the use of the *mailto* function is now widely implemented, allowing us to email page providers directly if we can't make sense of their offerings!

Search tools

For all that we have said above, one of the greatest benefits of the web is the proliferation of powerful search engines and directories for its resources. There are many of them both in the mainstream of use and under development: here we will focus on examples of the most important types -and try to highlight their differences, and what they can each best be used for. For convenience, I would categorise these types as the machine-generated indexes, the human-generated indexes, the metasearch or agent tools and the specialist indexes.

Machine-generated indexes

Machine-generated indexes and search tools, also often referred to as "spiders" or "crawlers" are systems such as Alta Vista and Webcrawler which involve only computers in the construction and indexing of their searchable databases, and have no direct human "control" over selection and indexing processes. They tend to be the largest, most comprehensive of the various engines in terms of coverage: indeed it used to be the case that the two main competitors of this type, Alta Vista and Lycos, constantly strove to outdo each other in terms of who had the biggest count of pages indexed on their home pages, a game which has thankfully petered out and been replaced by somewhat more helpful activities.

The principle behind the gathering and indexing of web pages by a tool of this sort is simple. Starting with a given page, after indexing its contents it will follow other URLs or links within the page, retrieving those pages and then performing a similar function on them in turn. Thus, in time, the system should harvest an enormous number of pages by simply following links from pages it has already indexed to new ones mentioned therein. Since all such systems also accept "suggestions" from individuals for new pages to look at (which are of course treated in the same manner) the crop of pages can indeed be bountiful. But within this system lies its own greatest weakness. It is so effective at garnering page references, that with more and more people creating more and more pages, inevitably the system eventually outstrips the capacity of its own machines to cope with the volume created. Whilst in the old days, as was noted, the count of pages indexed was seen as being the definition of greatness on such systems, now none trumpet their coverage in the same way. This is because they now regularly purge and reduce the number of pages listed in order to cope with the volumes concerned. Large, multi-item sites will find that only a proportion of their items are actually indexed; sites which seldom change their contents will find they are retrieved less and less. Whilst in theory these engines provide the most likely method for "indexing the web" in its entirety, in practice it is not practical for them to do so.

Further, the volume of data generated brings with it another problem of practical retrievability. Because the indexing method applied is essentially a free-text method, and the pool of data is so diverse, the classic problems of retrieval with natural language from large databases come into play. Whilst, due to its coverage and free-text indexing, the *recall* of these engines tends to be very high, their *precision* tends to be absolutely awful. Anyone who has used such engines will be familiar with searches commonly reporting hundreds of thousands of hits - not a very practical number to be wading through looking for the things we really want! Because the systems record every instance of the terms we use, and our terms can inevitably be used in so many contexts in a "database" as broad as the pool of web pages on the Internet, precision (or lack of it) becomes a real problem.

The systems do recognise this fact, and the specific mechanisms of their indexing do try to compensate for the problem by applying *relevance weighting* to their indexes in an attempt to improve precision. This means that, for instance, not only the occurrence of a word in a page is noted, but its position or nature is also noted, and the word is ranked as being more important if, for example, the word appears in a link, a heading or the title of a document. Other criteria of "importance" might be date of creation/access/amendment, frequency of the word's occurrence, or simply how far down the page it occurs. By recording not only the occurrence of a word but the importance of it in a page (as judged by this method), the system can first offer to the user those documents where the search terms are highly ranked (and therefore more relevant) rather than incidental. At least, that's the theory...

In practice, because these ranking systems are somewhat arbitrary, because the volumes of data are simply so great, and because in most cases the simplistic search interfaces users (who are expected to be novices, not information professionals) are presented with give them very little control over the search process, they fail miserably in their intention. They commonly present materials in which we have no interest as high-ranking, yet consign valuable materials to a place low down the list where most of us will never have the endurance to scan. They are badly flawed, and obscure in their actual operation. Indeed, the problems with the "enter-all-your terms-but-no-operators" basic interface commonly presented to the user, which normally selects documents containing *any* (Boolean OR) rather than *all* (Boolean AND) of the terms entered, and then promotes items if they contain more than one term, are particularly marked. Firstly, and astonishingly, they may actually not bother to return hits for certain terms you enter (because the documents containing them are so numerous), therefore immediately compromising their own approach by excluding important terms. For instance, a search for toxicological information systems would probably suppress the terms information and systems and return anything relating to toxicology - i.e. much which was nothing to do with information systems in that field. Secondly, since all terms are weighted, it is quite possible to end up with documents containing *fewer* of your terms appearing in the hit list before others that contain *more*. Take the time one day to scan down to the 20th page or so of results and you'll see what I mean - I guarantee you'll find things of far more relevance than many above them in the order. Thirdly, because the weighting mechanisms are opaque and hidden - it is very hard to find a meaningful description of exactly how they are applied - and vary from engine to engine, it is effectively impossible to tailor our queries to be more effective in the light of under-standing how they work.

So what can we in the information professions, who (hopefully!) know something more about searching and search techniques and tools than the average searcher, do to alleviate these problems and better employ our expertise? Well, there is good news and bad news. The good news is that most of these engines do have alternative interfaces (which may or may not be easy to find - follow any link which offers "search options" or "advanced searching") which allow more control over the search process - e.g. by the inclusion of Boolean operators or date limitation, often applied by check boxes. In fact, even the simple interfaces will usually accept instructions to use Boolean, phrase searching and other options - *if* you know how to specify them in the search language of the particular engine you are using. Always check out the help and search tips pages for any given engine - they may give you the wherewithal to greatly improve your searching efficiency.

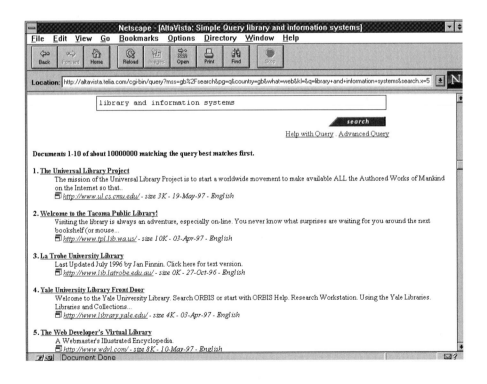

Figure 8: A search return from Alta Vista

The bad news is that, inevitably, there are absolute limitations to the efficiency of these systems (in terms of precision) which we must be aware of when trying to search. We cannot defeat the problems which naturally arise when searching for general information in a massive free-text index. The only answer is to use a different type of search tool for such enquiries, and limit our use of machine-generated indexes to highly specific queries (unless we want to spend a lot of time scanning through dross to find the occasional pearl!). There is an old adage that indexing effort is inversely proportional to search effort, which I like to think of as meaning human, rather than machine, effort. Which rather neatly brings us to the next category of search tool.

Human-generated indexes

Perhaps the term "human-generated index" is something of a misnomer, as the sites I am referring to in this category are systems such as Yahoo, although also those in less automated forms such as the WWW Virtual Library. These sites generally allow free-text searching, just as the machine-indexed sites do, but they add a layer of human control, organisation and selection of the data searched which makes them very different from the likes of the purely automated sites.

Essentially, the data in these systems is a considerably smaller proportion of the Internet's total output, with total pages numbering in thousands rather than millions (although the biggest do comprise several million entries - but still a tiny percentage of the biggest machine indexes which can reach 9 figures). At first glance this might be considered a drawback which it can be, in certain circumstances but there are two key differences in the way such systems work which more than offset this potential shortcoming. The first of these is the manner in which the sites indexed are selected for inclusion. Such sites are generally not, nor have ever intended to be, "comprehensive" in the sense of covering all web material. Rather they are deliberately *selective*, indexing only sites which human beings working in the companies consider worthy of inclusion. Their databases are grown and maintained by recommendation and evaluation of people rather than the purely mechanistic methods of the spiders. Not that this is a foolproof method, of course: I have found poor sites on Yahoo, and wondered at the non-appearance of good sites I have expected to find. However, on balance, it does mean that you tend to find more good material in such systems, if less overall.

Secondly, not only are the included sites actively selected for content, but they are also *classified*, indexed by humans and attributed to hierarchical categories which can be accessed as a subject tree as well as searched in full-text. A search on Yahoo at time of writing, for instance, will bring up multiple sets of results: firstly a list of the *categories* which contain the selected term(s), and secondly a list of the specific sites fulfilling the same criteria. Additionally, in this particular engine, if you don't generate many hits, the system also automatically passes on your search to Alta Vista and returns hits from there!

There are clear benefits in this approach. Firstly, as mentioned, much ephemeral and poor-quality material is weeded out at source, making the results more useful on the whole. Secondly, we can search effectively for broad or generalised topics and terms, as the human organisation will have identified and grouped such sites at appropriate levels in the hierarchy and we won't be deluged with hits as we would with the wider engines.

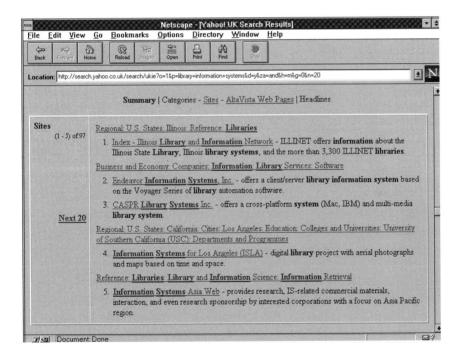

Figure 9: A search return from Yahoo

However, these tools are not perfect either. They generally offer only the simplest of interfaces, and just as with the machine-generated tools we have to hunt around for advanced search pages and help on more effective ways of narrowing and controlling our searches, which are usually available - so long as we can find them. As mentioned previously, their considerably smaller catchment can mean that useful things are easily missed, especially if we are looking for something complex and precise. And some people, especially in our professions, will doubtless complain about the conceptual weaknesses in the heirarchical structures, and the criteria for inclusion/exclusion of sites. Nevertheless, I would suggest they remain the prime source when searching for broad or generalised information.

Metasearch or agent tools

Both the preceding tool types have many sites which use them, and due to the idiosyncracies of coverage and weighting, if we want breadth we often have to try more than one such tool. A relatively recent development which aims to assist us in broadening our scope whilst keeping up precision are metasearch tools, or agent tools as they are sometimes called a metasearch tool, as the name implies, is not a search tool in itself, but a tool which knows about other search tools, such as Metafind and Dogpile. You construct a search which your metasearch tool then resubmits to a number of other tools and systems (most vary from 3-20 systems), and then analyses, orders and represents the returns to you according to your specifications.

Because they search across a number of other sources, there are limitations to how effective they can be in their searching, as features which are not supported in any of the destination search engines can obviously not be used, which tends to push users to adopt a "lowest common denominator" approach. However, they can be very helpful in gathering information on the most useful (or perhaps one should say, *apparently* most useful) sites for any given topic.

Most of these engines work on the principle of taking the highest-ranking hits from the various engines they pass their requests on to, limiting their selection either by number of hits or sometimes by time elapsed in response. Results can then usually be grouped either by site, keyword, or other parameters, allowing the user to easily analyse what has appeared where and how it has been ranked. This is a very easy way of broadening coverage but minimising the effect of massive recall killing off precision: key sites will hopefully appear in more than one system and thus be flagged up, but lesser-known sites should still appear on at least one system near the top if truly relevant. As is the case with all the systems, it is not a 100% reliable method, and oddities can still crop up and good sites fail to appear, but the approach offers a good compromise between the recall overkill of the machine indexes and the narrower view of the human indexes. In particular, the flexible nature of the selection of sites to check and of the display of results can enable the experienced searcher to gain thorough but easy-to-evaluate reporting of suitable sites.

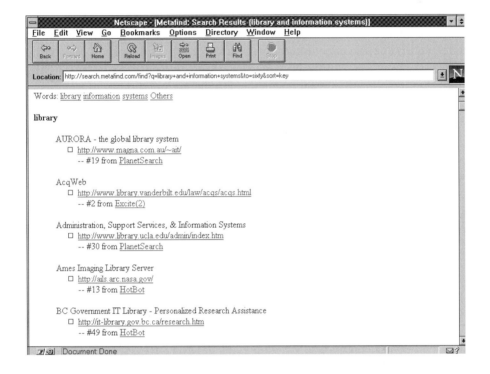

Figure 10: A search return from Metafind

Specialist indexes

One of the most interesting and in my view, logical developments has been the rise of what I term the specialist index or gateway. These are directories of Internet resources in particular subject areas, compiled and organised by specialists and information professionals in their respective fields, which typically represent the best of sites available in the field concerned. Whilst the concept of the subject tree has been with us for many years, and whilst within those general subject trees some excellent subject specialisms have flourished (and often, specific subject trees come to be known for their particular strength in such areas), it is only in the last couple of years that interest has developed in building single-subject sites as centres of excellence in referencing the Internet at large.

Nowadays there are a considerable number of such indexes available, such as OMNI (Organising Medical Networked Information), EEVL (Edinburgh Engineering Virtual Library), SOSIG (Social Sciences Information Gateway) and the like. Whilst these specialist sites do not replace the traditional broad-scope sites and gateways like BUBL and NISS, they do represent a valuable trend in both the conservation of effort and in the promotion of quality for information referencing on the Internet. Like any human-controlled collection, they are not flawless and cannot contain every worthy site, but they do carry with them a certain stamp of authority and tend to be kept up-to-date to a far greater extent than some other such sites. A visit to this sort of resource is almost mandatory if you are looking for information in a field for which such an index exists. Some are listed in the resource guide in this book, but as new sites develop, you would be best advised to check online for new ones in the broader gateways such as NISS and BUBL, where you ought to find them listed in current form.

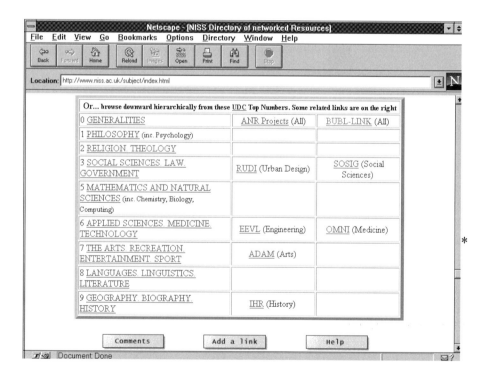

Figure 11: Some specialist gateways at NISS

General points on searching

As can be drawn from the above descriptions, there follow a number of points which can be taken as good generalised suggestions to bear in mind whilst searching on the WWW. Firstly, the best form of search depends very much on the type of enquiry you have to fulfil. If the topic is a complex one which requires a number of conceptual "keywords" to cover it, then starting your search in broad-based, machine-indexed tool like Alta Vista is probably your best bet, as precision should be enhanced if you use a lot of keywords. On the other hand, if the topic is a broad or generalised one which can be described in only one or two words, you are almost certainly better off starting with a more selective directory-based tool like Yahoo. Likewise, if you need exhaustivity, go for the machine-indexed tools, but if you simply need one or two good sources, try the directories. If you're taking the directory approach, see if a specialist gateway exists for your subject area, and try that. If you're not sure of which approach to take, or you want a balance, or a broad view across multiple sites without being swamped, try the metasearch engines.

Some tools are now also making compromises toward other types: e.g. Yahoo's automatic running of a search on Alta Vista if it finds few hits on its own, or Lycos' "top 250" which lists sites most referenced by others (and therefore, it is assumed, most popular) and its A2Z categorisation of sites.

Always make a point of seeking out the advanced search interfaces on all tools, and checking out the help for the correct command syntax to implement the sorts of search we are used to being able to make with traditional online hosts - all those engines have a command language if you can only find a definition of it! Some such pages which exist at time of writing are listed in the resource guide, but they may well have changed between my writing this and your reading it - in my experience, the major search engines all seem to totally reconstruct their sites several times a year! - so do check, check and check again online. In particular, note that the best information may not be immediately apparent - you may have to go several layers to find it. And on that note, apply the same principle to search results returned - don't just look at the first page of output, check some subsequent pages as well, the weaknesses of the ranking algorithms in the engines may well obscure good hits by scoring them artificially low.

Other Web developments

Where to begin? So much is going on in this field it's impossible to be even superficially comprehensive in a guide of this kind, much less to write something which will look up-to-date even six months from publication. Perhaps I should first mention some things people might *expect* me to be writing about, and say a few words on why I haven't prioritised them.

The most obvious place to start in this fashion must be to say something about *Java*. Five years ago, when the Internet was first becoming a mass-market phenomenon, the hype was all about "The Internet". Everyone had heard of it but few had experienced it, and it was talked up like crazy. Five years on, enough people have experienced the Internet that we really do have some understanding of what it is and we can tell when it's being oversold. I feel to some extent we're in a similar situation with Java - everyone's heard of it, everyone's been told how wonderful and important it is and how they can't do without it, but few people are actually in a sufficiently informed position about it to know when things are being overstated.

Java is actually a programming language, developed by Sun. It has two main significances: firstly, it is being touted as a platform-independent language, and secondly (usually in the form of Javascript) that it can be used to do all sorts of fancy things with web pages which ordinary HTML can't do. However I see two problems related to these points which in my view dramatically reduce the true value and impact of Java to the Internet community.

Firstly with regard to its platform independence. The idea behind this is that Java itself is written to run on a "virtual" Java machine, which would be the same everywhere. Individual computing systems would have programs which would take care of converting the Java code into something which could actually be executed on any given real-world machine. Thus anyone writing a Java program or applet could have confidence that it would work anywhere.

Well, pardon my cynicism, but this is the computer industry we're dealing with here. And any of you readers who have done a little computing in the past might just hear some bells ringing... Whatever happened to Pascal for instance? Wasn't that a programming language which was supposed to be machine-independent, producing a thing called p-code which could then be used on any machine by running another program to convert it to the machine code any real-world machine needed?

But in reality, Pascal programs are not totally portable, and what works on one system doesn't work on another - only real lowest-common-denominator things are even moderately portable. The same is true in the operating system side with Unix, originally given away and intended to be a universal tool but now existing in a great many (largely incompatible) incarnations. Businesses look for competitive advantage, which you don't get from base standards, no matter how much they might benefit the end-user. In all fairness I should point out here that my view would not be shared by all commentators, but nevertheless I make the point for your consideration. However even if we assume for the moment that I am wrong in this negative assumption, it does not circumvent the second shortcoming.

On then to the *application* of Java to web pages. As you have seen, HTML, the "normal" method for creating web pages, lacks many abilities web page producers would like it to have. It cannot give total control to the producer over what the user sees: it cannot handle fancy effects and devices: and perhaps most importantly, if a producer wants a level of *interaction* with the user of a page, that interaction is very limited and must be handled by what is called *server-side processing* - in short, all an HTML page can do is gather some data, pass it back to the server, which can then process the data in some way and return another HTML page to the user. An example of this is the action of a search engine: you enter data (search terms) in an HTML-based "form", which is transmitted to the appropriate server. A program running on the server then takes the data and translates it into a search statement for the actual database program at the host's end, and submits it: the search is performed, the results fed back to the program on the server which then repackages the results in HTML and sends it back to your client for display - and you see the results. So, nearly all the work of processing is done at the server's end, and virtually none at your client's end.

Java offers the prospect of *client-side processing*: i.e that more of the processing effort could be done at the client's end, thus lessening the load on the server. A Java-based program included on a web page can run and do many things, all at the user's end, without reference to the server. This allows many things in theory, such as far more interactive, helpful data entry and pre-processing, the creation and display of many fancy special effects, and a system which can make appropriate responses and invoke actions based on the choices and options a user makes.

All of this is fine in theory, and all it requires (given the consistency we have previously discussed) is that the client's browser can cope with Java - and that it allows it to. Firstly it is wise to remember that many older versions of browsers cannot cope with Java (there is an awful assumption that the latest technology is what everybody has, which is simply untrue). But more importantly, even if it can cope with Java - will it be allowed to?

The obvious response would be, "well, why not?". In fact, many, many Java-capable browsers are regularly run with their Java capability turned off - and for good reason. There is a big difference between loading and viewing an HTML page and using Java. With HTML, you are simply loading and interpreting data. Control of your system rests at all times with your browser, and *nothing* you download is anything but data used by that browser at that time. When you load a page with Java in it, you are *running a program*, which in effect takes control of your system. And whilst data alone cannot harm your system, a running program certainly can. If you are at all concerned about virus protection (and if you're not, you should be!) you will be aware that the first rule is never to run a program you haven't virus-checked! Browsers supporting Java open a gaping hole in any system's defences against attack from the outside. Much is made by the proponents of Java of the "sandbox" concept, which is supposed to isolate Java programs from the rest of your system, but in many peoples' view it is still very insecure. My personal view is that anyone running a Java-enabled browser is either brave, or foolhardy.

There are certainly potential benefits to be had from some improved client-side processing, but the final nail in the coffin from my perspective is that much of the use of Java (to date) has been ephemeral, particularly for visual effects. Until the security problems are sorted out, and until providers become much more mature in their use of the technology, Java will remain something the developers will be keen on, but which I believe the intelligent public will largely reject.

In some way related to the Java debate is the concept of *real-time updating*, "server push" and "client pull". This reflects the desire of some services to use the Internet as a medium for passing information in an active way, rather than relying on the passive model which the current state of web pages represents. In other words, at the moment, and information provider creates a web page, but is then reliant on the *user* to come an get it: the provider has no control over when the user gets the page, sees an update etc. Likewise, if a user fetches a page containing, say, share price information or some other volatile piece of data, that data may change even in the space of time the user is looking at the page, but those changes won't be reflected. What is desired is a system where such changes are automatically notified to the user, or which will give the provider a means to transmit to the user at a time of their (provider's) choosing. Expect more developments in this area, but again I feel it is something of a red herring. Systems which truly *require* this sort of real-time update already exist outside the Internet for serious users: it strikes me that once more this is a development which lacks true value for most end-users, once the resources it might consume are taken into account. One of my current pet hates are pages which regularly recall servers for reload information (a form of "client pull"), eating bandwidth and interfering with my concentration at this end.

Another buzzword at present is *metadata*, which is really one more for providers than users of information, but which does have some potential for us. All web pages can have metadata (="data about data") tags attached to them, indicating such things as indexing keywords the authors wish to have used, descriptions of content etc. Most good search engines take account of this data in their indexing and weighting. If you are involved in producing as well as searching for web-based information, do check them out and make use of them. However, they can be valuable in providing search terms, much as in traditional online searching we might review the indexing which had been applied to a document in order to find more like it, the so-called "pearl-growing" technique of searching. Whilst using this method on the web is less reliable than in traditional onliine, as most engines do not allow us to restrict our searches to metadata tag fields, and of course there is no control over the authors' use of terms, it can be helpful to review such data in documents we find are good ones. You can easily do this by selecting the "view source" option in your browser - the meta tags are all in the "head" block which comes at the beginning of each page.

Agents are also much talked about at present. We have said something about these in passing when discussing metasearch tools. Agents are sometimes painted as being software programs which can be given parameters about our particular interests, or examples of things we like, and then set loose to scour the web for more material we want. They are particularly talked of in the context of mailing lists and newsgroups, but also more generally. The consensus on agents seems to be, at least at present, that they are largely a waste of time. Quite apart from failing to accurately report material on users' needs, they consume large amounts of bandwidth, adding further to the congestion problem of the net. Further, one might question the very principle of relying on agent-retrieved data: often the general or unknown is of interest to us even though it is off our primary topic. If we were to rely too much on an agent (assuming it worked) it would be like receiving a daily newspaper which only told us what we expected to hear. Many lists and newsgroups have a deliberately wide scope to encourage cross-fertilisation of ideas and awareness of new topics. An agent-based approach inhibits these valuable features.

Web interfaces are now also commonly available to all the other tools we have mentioned earlier: Archie, Veronica and WAIS all have web-based front-ends we can use, and are often available for other information sources on the Internet.

Error messages also deserve a mention, because they are mostly so unhelpful. One of the most common I tend to see nowadays which is particularly misleading is one which reports "DNS entry not found" or something similar, suggesting you have entered an erroneous URL. Generally this is not the case! If you try again with exactly the same URL a few seconds later, you will find that nine times out of ten you can now connect quite happily. This is because the routing of requests requires the *IP address* of the destination server, which is a string of numbers, not a text name. In order to convert your name ("www.host.com" or whatever) into an address (something like "127.221.58.101" perhaps) the system uses a Domain Name Server (DNS) which provides the matchup. However local DNS can't hold all the names in use around the world: but if it's asked for one it doesn't know, it asks other servers if they know. Once it gets an answer, it remembers it for a time. Thus your error message usually means "sorry, don't have a note of this" rather than an actual "this doesn't exist". Unfortunately, that's not how it looks. In fact, many of the final-looking error messages will actually disappear if you simply wait a few moments and retry: they are often caused by one form or another of network congestion (the DNS message above can also sometimes be caused by this) or shortage of local information. So the moral of this part of the story is definitely: if at first you don't succeed, try, try again!

When it comes to ultimately deciding which search tools to use for what, it really isn't possible to say in a *definitive* manner "use this for this and that for that" beyond the generalisations I have already made, even before we try to take account of the rate of change in this area: Here as in the rest of information retrieval from the Internet, there is no substitute for trying out in order to really find out. You need to monitor developments, experiment and practice, and to keep on doing so, to be able to search the web effectively.

Although I have tried throughout this book to avoid giving references to specific resources for fear of their becoming obsolete, I feel the need to mention one extremely valuable resource here, as at time of writing it has no peer as a single source of information on developments in web searching and the like. This is the Search Engine Report by Calafia, a (currently) free mailing-list-based service which sends substantial, regular reports on general search engine news for both developers and searchers, and its companion website Search Engine Watch. If you want to keep up with search engine developments, this is the list to sign up with!

Key tips for the effective use of the World Wide Web:

- Make constant use of bookmarks to create a personal resource guide
- Don't trust data without checking its provenance
- Don't allow Java applications to run on your browser unchecked
- Configure your browser to use other applications
- When saving pages, watch out for relative links which will cease to work
- URLs change: check regularly to see they're still OK
- Use machine-indexed tools like Alta Vista for the widest possible coverage
- Use human-indexed directories like Yahoo for quicker, subject-based needs
- Use Metasearch tools like Metafind to get a broad view without being deluged
- Use the advanced search forms in all tools to give more control over searching
- Be prepared to invest time "surfing" to find useful sites
- Don't give up if you get an error message - try again
- Subscribe to the Search Engine Watch mailing list
- Things change rapidly - keep trying out new options!

9. Summary/Conclusions

We've surveyed lot of ground in what is only a very short book, but I hope that even in this brief look at what the Internet is, and the tools we currently have to use with it for information retrieval, it has become clear that the Net is far from the won-drous information panacea that the media so often hold it up to be - it certainly cannot currently be relied upon as a reference tool.

That said, I also hope that you recognise that the Internet still represents a valuable resource to add to the more traditional sources we have always used. Like any other resource the key to its effective use is to capitalise on its strengths and recognise its weaknesses. Likewise, with the various tools we have to use on the Net, we need to constantly be aware of how they're working, how they differ from the expectations we might have of them - brought from our experiences with traditional online systems, for instance - and what they are and are not good at doing. Just because something's imperfect doesn't mean we can't get some benefit out of what it can do; and if the current tools are imperfect, let's not forget that new tools, new approaches, new ideas are constantly being developed to give us better ways of identifying and retrieving material from the Net.

One problem which will never go away, however, is the sheer size of the data resource accessible by the Internet, and the difficulties that creates for searching and identifying information on a global scale. I personally believe this will be solved not by some great new technological advance, but by a change in the users' ap-proach, to a more locally-based method of information retrieval.

After all, forgetting the Internet for a moment, if we want some information, what is the typical pattern of our search for it? I would suggest, we look for things closest to home first, and always have done. We buy books on the subjects that interest us; if we want something, we look first to our personal, local resources. If it's not on our shelves, we may ask a friend. Next we'd go to the local branch library. If that branch doesn't have it, they'd search elsewhere in their regional system for it. If there was still no joy, they'd try to borrow from a national and then international source. Alternatively, if what we were looking for was specialist in some way, we might approach a specialist institution or society at some stage in the above cycle (or indeed at more than one stage). The point is, most of the time we don't, search the whole world's resources to find something which satisfies our needs. We use local and specialised focal points to help us.

With the image of the Internet as a world-wide, global thing (which it is) we seem to have also inherited an expectation that we should be always searching in a global fashion, simply because we have the notional ability to connect to all parts of it. Yet how often in a "normal" search for information do we feel the need to be so exhaustive? And in the "normal" environment, how much of our time as information professionals do we spend collating, indexing, advising and assisting users as to the quickest, most economic method to find what they want?

As others have started to suggest, I believe our role in relation to the Internet will become more and more that of gatekeepers, organisers of links to information on the Net, and that the focus of these access-providing activities will be far less global (although not without far-reaching links). We will become more and more the providers of organised, select sets of pointers to original data sources, translating our traditional role of organisers of local physical resources into organisers of local links to remote resources. Some have complained about the proliferation of individual and institutional subject trees and clamour for a single, monolithic method of finding resources on the Internet. I applaud and encourage this distributed building of selected and locally tailored assistance, and suggest it is the way things will inevitably continue. Already we can see signs of this happening: most of the major search engines are now touting "local" (country-based) versions of their sites with local resources highlighted, and as we have mentioned many high-quality subject-specialised gateways have sprung into being, mostly designed and maintained by people in the library and information profession (OMNI, EEVL, SOSIG).

The Internet will not be, as many have suggested, the greatest revolution in information dissemination since Gutenberg's press. History reveals we have an extraordinary tendency to exaggerate the future importance of such developments. For instance, in the forties, people were speaking in *exactly* the same terms about the development of - microfilm. Microfilm has been an extremely useful addition to the range of information media we use, but it has not supplanted all else - and nor will use of the Internet, although it will be a significant addition to our existing methods. And it will certainly evolve, indeed is already evolving, into a very useful mainstream communications medium as and when it surmounts the current problems of congestion and penetration from which it currently suffers. The gap between the information rich and poor is exaggerated not only by access to kit and skills, but by access to infrastructure, e.g. in Africa. I don't believe this will continue to be such a major problem in the long term, but it will for the next ten years or so, and it will never go away entirely.

But this is looking to the future. For now, we must be aware of the weaknesses in the current tools, accept them, and use them within their limitations. Yes, there are very real difficulties in quickly, accurately finding answers on the Internet, and yet at the same time the answers to almost every question may be out there somewhere. For now, we must continue to labour under the uncertainty of quality of information we find, the imprecision of the tools, and the sheer volumes of redundant information on the Net. It is not, and never will be, a fully organised, controlled place. But if we accept the need to invest time, even to "waste" time "surfing", and use that experience to create our *own*, somewhat more stable and organised points of access to the best that we find, if we take back that role of guide and intermediary we have lately been in fear of losing to "end-user access" and to the computer people and their tools, I think we will find much of considerable value and use, and much to be thankful for in the Internet. We have a real opportunity here to re-establish the importance of our traditional skills in organising, describing and helping people to be able to quickly retrieve information, in this new and exciting context, and to reclaim our professional role which has been so usurped by the technologists over the past twenty years. Let's not waste the opportunity.

And we'll have a lot of fun exploring into the bargain!

Appendix

Further reading

Eddings, J. How the Internet works. Ziff-Davis, Emery CA, 1994

Hahn, H. The Internet complete reference. 2nd ed Osbourne McGraw-Hill, Berkeley, CA 1996

<u>Internet World</u> magazine

Pride, S. Email for librarians. ASLIB, London, 1994

Resource list

As you should now be aware, resources on the Internet are in a constant state of flux. Today's list of good sites is tomorrow's list of connections refused! Thus I have tried to present here simply a handful of suggestions of key sites, lists or resources which are unlikely to be as volatile as the average, and in particular to point you at starting points from which to find resources rather than always at the resources themselves. I cannot guarantee that all the things listed below will be available as noted when you read this; however, I hope that the great majority of them will still be even some years from the time of writing. If you cannot reach a particular resource as noted below, please don't blame me, or yourself - it's just the nature of the Internet!

Mailing lists and groups

The lis-link and lis-series lists on library and information science are held at Mailbase. To get a list of these lists by email post to mailbase@mailbase.ac.uk with a message "find lists lis" (or just one word "lists" for *all* Mailbase lists).

For Listserv servers, ask "list global". you can suffix your request "/subject" where subject is the thing you're interested in.

General lists of lists can be had by FTP from various sources, including SRI/NISC (ftp.nisc.sri.com) and Dartmouth University, New Hampshire (dartcms1.dartmouth.edu). But BEWARE! These lists are VERY big.

Generally it's much better to use web-based interfaces to lists of mail lists and newsgroups such as Mailbase, Liszt and Deja News (details below) if you can.

Useful sources

The sources listed below are given as standard URLs for use in a browser such as Netscape. If you do not have such a browser and want to access e.g. a telnet source with a telnet client, simply elide the first element of the URL. Thus, to access RSL's OPAC list by telnet (URL telnet://rsl.ox.ac.uk) open rsl.ox.ac.uk in your telnet client.

Alta Vista:

Home page:	http://www.altavista.digital.com
Advanced search:	http://www.altavista.digital.com/cgi-bin/query?pg=aq
	(check help before using!)
UK version:	

http://altavista.telia.com/

    cgi-bin/query?pg=q&country=gb&mss=gb%2Fsearch&x=29&y=22

Archie:

Imperial College:	Telnet//archie.doc.ic.ac.uk
Internic (New Jersey):	Telnet//archie.internic.net
Archieplexform (web-based)	http://src.doc.ic.ac.uk/archieplexform.html

Ask A Librarian:

email:	answers@earl.org.uk
webinterface:	http://www.earl.org.uk/earl/web/ask.htm

BUBL:

Home page	http://www.bubl.ac.uk
Subject tree (BUBL LINK)	
Gopher:	gopher://bubl.bath.ac.uk:7070
Deja News:	http://www.dejanews.com

FTP sites:

HENSA (software)	FTP//micros.hensa.ac.uk (for micro-based)
	FTP//unix.hensa.ac.uk (for UNIX-based)

Imperial:	FTP//src.doc.ic.ac.uk:70/1

Hytelnet:

Geographical list of OPACS:	telnet//rsl.ox.ac.uk (now needs personal login)
Web interface:	http://www.cam.ac.uk/Hytelnet/ index.html

The Internet Public Library: http://ipl.sils.umich.edu

Liszt: http://www.liszt.com

Lycos:

Home page:	http://www.lycos.com
UK version:	http://www-uk.lycos.com
Custom search:	

http://www-uk.lycos.com/assist-uk/pages/customsearch.html

Metafind: http://www.metafind.com

Mailbase: Mailbase@mailbase.ac.uk

Web interface: http://www.mailbase.ac.uk

Netscape search tool page:

http://home.netscape.com/escapes/search/netsearchv1.html

NISS gateway: telnet//niss.ac.uk

Web interface: http://www.niss.ac.uk

Public access gophers:

gopher.brad.ac.uk	Bradford University (login as GOPHER)
gopher.msu.edu	Michigan State University (login as GOPHER)

The Search Engine report: majordomo@calafia.com

(send message "subscribe searchreport")

Search Engine Watch: http://searchenginewatch.com

Stumpers-L mailing list:	mailserv@crf.cuis.edu
	(send message "subscribe stumpers-l")
Veronica:	
Manchester server:	gopher://veronica.mcc.ac.uk:2347/7
Index of Veronica servers:	gopher://gopher/scs.unr.edu/11/veronica
SUNET (Sweden)	gopher://veronica.sunet.se:2347/7
PSI (California)	gopher://gopher.psi.com:2347/7
The Virtual Library:	http://www.w3.org/hypertext/DataSources/ by Subject/Overview
WAIS:	
Public clients:	telnet://wais@quake.think.com/
	telnet://wais@wais.com
Directory of servers:	wais://wais.com:210/
Web interface	http://www.ai.mit.edu/the-net/wais.html
Yahoo:	
Home page:	http://www.yahoo.com/
UK version:	http://www.yahoo.co.uk
Search options:	http://search.yahoo.co.uk/search.ukie/ options

Short glossary

agent: a software program which performs tasks for a user; usually relating to the gathering of predefined types of information.

applet: a "little application" (app-let), normally written in Java/javascript (q.v.); a program which can be embedded in a web page.

ASCII: American Standard Code for Information Interchange. The most universal code for converting data signals into the text we see on the screen.

browser: a client program for accessing Internet resources. Most commonly used to refer to a client for the WWW.

BUBL: the Bulletin Board for Libraries, an important LIS gateway (q.v.)

client: a program which runs on a local machine, controlling local display, input and output functions, and communications with a server on a remote host for the retrieval of data.

client pull: a mechanism by which a client can automatically reload updated information for a page on a regular basis.

CWIS: Campus-Wide Information System.

distributed system: a system in which processing is performed at multiple locations rather than in a single machine.

EARL: Electronic Access to Resources in Libraries: a UK consotium for public library networking

FAQ: Frequently Asked Questions. FAQ files provide basic information on the topics they relate to in the form of previously asked questions and the answers thereto. Commonly produced by newsgroups.

gateway: a site or system which provides access to other sites or systems as its primary function.

GUI: Graphical User Interface. A point-and-click type of interface, such as Windows, as opposed to a text-based Command Line Interface.

HENSA: the Higher Education National Software Archive at Lancaster, major FTP site for software in the UK.

HotJava: a proprietary page editing and creation tool for working with the Java (q.v.) page layout language produced by Sun.

HTML: HyperText Mark-up Language. The basic language used in preparing pages for the WWW.

HTTP: HyperText Transfer Protocol.

Java: a proprietary programming language produced by Sun.

Javascript: a subset of Java used for producing programs to run inside web pages (see applet).

line mode: a text-based connection between computers, commonly used for dial-up connections.

mailto: a tag used in HTML which links to an email facility, enabling the reader of a page to send email to a specified recipient by simply selecting it.

Nettiquette: the term for the code of conduct expected of Internet users. A contraction of "Network Etiquette".

NISS: National Information Systems and Services, a gateway (q.v.) to many information services for HE

node: a connection point, e.g. to a network

packet: a basic "chunk" of data transmitted across a network. A file can be broken down into a number of packets for transmission, each packet proceeding independently, and then reassembled into a file at the receiving end.

packet-switching: the method employed to pass packets across the telecommunications system by variable routes.

PDF: Portable Document Format, a proprietary page layout language system produced by Adobe.

PPP: Point to Point Protocol. A protocol commonly used for establishing a full connection to the Internet via a telephone and modem link.

protocol: a definition or standard describing how computers will act when communicating with each other.

Remote login: logging into a computer at another site from your local terminal, which then acts as if it was a terminal at that site.

RFC: Request For Comment. RFC files contain discussion of and information on the standards and proposed standards of the Internet.

router: a device which transfers data between two or more networks which use the same protocols, but which may be physically different.

RTFM: "Read The F****** Manual!". An all too commonly used acronymic expletive.

server: a program which runs on a machine, organising data and responding to requests from client programs for access to that data. Also, in common usage, the machine on which such a program runs.

server push: a mechanism by which a server can automatically reload updated information to a client for a page.

SGML: Standard Generalised Mark-up Language.

SLIP: Serial Line Internet Protocol. A protocol commonly used for establishing a full connection from a PC to the Internet via a telephone and modem link.

TCP/IP: Transmission Control Protocol/Internet Protocol. The basic protocols on which all Internet communication is founded.

URL: Uniform Resource Locator. A standard format for describing the type and location of an information resource to be accessed over the Internet, most commonly via the WWW.

Usenet: The largest grouping of public newsgroups, based in the USA, (in)famous for the scope and weirdness of some of its groups.

Z39.50: An ANSI standard for the request and transmission of bibliographic and related data.